# SWEET LOVE

Grandmas Timeless Dessert Recipes
That Reconnect Cultural Traditions

Iman Osman

My mother and grandmother.

My grandma originally gifted these
recipes to my mom with the dedication:

*"To my dear daughter Hoda,
from mom Neamat."* 1973
(the original dedication is written in
Arabic image on previous page)

As I publish this book, I dedicate it to my
sweet baby Hoda and my shining star niece
Rashda. May you grow to be the most
beautiful souls, just like your great-grandma.

Me and my neice Rashda.

I would like to thank my mother, without whom this book wouldn't exist. My father, for always supporting encouraging and believing in me. This book would never come to life without an amazing team who has supported in every way. From the amazing food photographer, Ahmed Osos who has been so patient and supportive to Engy Mosleh who took on the styling of the photos to a whole new level and has been truly helpful and patient at every step. Our amazing pastry chefs, Chef Maged Hussien and Sawsan Hassan, for bringing all their talent and creativity in crafting all the products for the photo shoot and for the hours spent converting recipe measurements. A special thanks to Katherine Sombol for the precious memories she captured of my family. I am forever grateful for the beautiful photos. Last but definitely not the least, a special thank you to Moustafa Hamwi and the entire Passionpreneur team, who have been so patient with me and guided me through the entire process. This book has been a dream on my mind for years and you guys really made it come to life.

# Contents

My grandmother.

# Introduction

The *whirrrr* of the grinding machine. The *thwack-thwack* of a hand-whisk. The *clickety-click* of the oven timer. And the aroma of whatever was baking in that oven. These make up some of my favourite childhood memories. I remember walking in to our house from school to find grandma sitting on *her* chair in the kitchen – "Too old to stand for too long," she'd say – instructing her helpers, a cook for savouries and a baker for desserts, on what to stir and what to pour.

All my mom and uncles' birthdays, my mother tells me, were unparalleled feasts, filled with interesting sandwiches and many different kinds of cake – from sponge cakes with fruits to chocolate cake, jelly cakes, trifle and homemade pastries. She made everything from scratch, right down to getting the freshest cream straight from the milkman. Birthday buffets back then were a very different thing, I'm told!

Birthdays aside, every day was a treat. Even the sandwiches that went into my mother's and her brother's daily lunch boxes were baked and assembled from scratch. Their breakfast table, mother recalls, would always have a special pastry she called 'kafafy' that they would eat with honey or homemade jam.

Mother reminisces about how the fragrance from their kitchen would waft through the entire building and how all the neighbours, especially the British ones on the same floor, would get to eat grandma's baking. These, of course, were times when the tradition of sharing with the neighbours was well-respected and followed.

Not only was my grandmother a great baker, she was also always very well turned out – well dressed, taking care of herself and making sure her kitchen was spotless, even as she baked up a storm!

My grandmother's dining room. Now that in itself is a treat to remember. The long, beautiful 16-seater dining table and its matching buffet and mirror. The table was so big that she was never able to find ready-made table cloths for it. She always had to have them custom-made. And she got some really elegant ones done. There were always vases filled with pretty flowers. My mother still has her favourite table cloth and a well-loved vase which she continues to fill with pretty flowers, much like my grandmother did in her days. My grandmother sure was creative and had good taste, in more ways than one.

I remember getting very excited about the hand-held mixer, fascinated as the runny egg-whites turned into tiny mountains, their heads held high; waiting to line up the pastry sheets to make the baklava; standing with my eyes glued to the oven, waiting for the cake to rise; and best of all, polishing off the cake batter clinging to the bowl. I don't think anything can ever come close to those moments, those experiences and the bond it created between my grandma, my mother and me. Simpler, happier times – in my grandma's and my mother's kitchen.

What came out of that kitchen, onto our tables and into our eagerly waiting hands is what this book is made of. Some of the pictures in this book will also give you a peek of that wonderful dining table and of some of my grandmother's beautiful, ornate cutlery.

While this book is my grandmother's gift to my mother – she made so many recipes for my mother and compiled them – it is also my endeavour to bring alive that love, that togetherness that we all may have lost along the way thanks to the busy lives we lead. I connected with my grandma thanks to food, and that bond runs deep. This book is my way of bringing my own kids and my mother together over our shared love for food; for the timeless desserts that my grandmother has passed down to us.

This book, a compilation of dessert recipes across seasons, is also my way to help Middle Eastern – and other – mothers aspiring to bring back family bonds that have been lost in today's fast-paced world so they can reconnect with their cultural traditions.

Even though I run my own food-related business, this book brings together the personal experiences of my very traditional Middle Eastern family. These recipes have been experimented with, have had our own flavours added to them and have been tried and tested through generations before being passed down to me. I am now happy to bring together this compilation of love for you.

To (mis)quote Shakespeare's – "If desserts be the food of love, read on!"

My grandmother.

# How to read this book

When I asked my mother to help me out with this book, she spoke of each recipe in connection to one of the four seasons. The way she looked and how her voice changed with the description of each season is the inspiration behind sectioning the book into seasons.

Each season has its own charm and its own taste. Ingredients available in a particular season are traditionally best suited to that time of the year. You will find recipes for all four major seasons in the book.

I have strived to create the book in such a way that you can start making desserts from any season. There is also a section on basic recipes. These are the recipes that you will find being repeatedly used across the seasons.

If you are a new baker, there is a section on general tips for you. If you are a seasoned baker, there are variations in a lot of recipes that we have enjoyed and that you may want to experiment with.

Conversions usually confound us and sometimes even change a recipe and how it tastes. You will find measurements in grams as well as cups in my book. I have tested all the conversions by hand, rechecking them many times because when I searched for conversions I didn't find a standard one. Many sources gave me different results, so I decided to do it myself. For convenience, I have rounded up or down when converting, and have tested all the recipes with both conversions to make sure they will get you the same results whichever measurement system you use.

I hope you enjoy the process of creating the dessert, as much as you and your loved ones enjoy the taste of it.

# General tips

## STAGES OF WHIPPING EGG WHITES OR HEAVY CREAM

**SOFT PEAK** After beating for about 30 seconds, remove the whisk handle from the mixer and turn it upside down. If the peaks are just starting to hold but fall off the whisk and melt back into foam, then this is a soft peak.

**FIRM PEAK** Turn the whisk handle upside down. If the peaks hold and are more visible, but you find the tips falling off the whisk, this is a firm peak.

**STIFF PEAK** You won't need to turn the whisk to check. Once the mixture is thick, the peaks will hold themselves and point straight up without collapsing at all.

### GHEE REPLACEMENTS

In any recipe that calls for ghee, clarified butter is the only replacement. Nothing else will get the same result. Unless stated otherwise.

Flatten the bean on a cutting board.

Using a small sharp knife, slice it in half through the middle.

Do not cut through the centre as this will cause you to lose a lot of the vanilla pods.

Once you slice it, scrape out all the pods inside from both sides with the back of the knife.

If you are using a bag of vanilla beans, once the bag is open, make sure you reseal it, taking all the air out to make sure they don't dry out.

Place the cake on a flat surface.

To split a cake, use a serrated knife. Use the knife to mark the thickness you want each layer to be and make sure you mark it all the way around the cake.

Hold the knife parallel to the work surface and cut through the cake slowly, constantly checking that you are slicing where you marked.

If you are cutting more than 1 layer, make sure to cover the layers already cut and set aside so that they don't dry out.

# Basic
# Recipes

# Whipped Chocolate Ganache

Whipped chocolate ganache is an incredibly rich and decadent frosting.

**SERVING SIZE**
Enough to fill a kg of chocolate sablé or to fill and decorate a 24 cm (9.5 in) cake

| bittersweet chocolate | 400 g | 2 cups |
|---|---|---|
| heavy cream | 300 ml | 1¼ cups |

Finely chop the chocolate and place in a large heat-proof bowl.

Bring cream to a boil over medium-high heat.

Pour directly over chopped chocolate. Allow to sit for a couple of minutes.

Use a rubber spatula or a small whisk to gently stir chocolate and cream until the chocolate is totally melted and combined.

Cool completely, while stirring continuously.

Once cooled, place it in the refrigerator to chill.

When ready to use, whip the ganache with a wire whisk or a hand-held electric mixer with the whisk attachment until it begins to hold its shape.

**TIPS AND TRICKS**

*Be careful not to overwhip it as it can become grainy.*

*The ganache will keep thickening after you stop whisking.*

*Don't whip the ganache unless you are using it right away. That way, the ganache will be fluffy when you serve the dessert.*

**SERVING AND STORING SUGGESTIONS**

You can use whipped ganache for biscuit or cake fillings and to decorate cakes.

Once the ganache is done, it can last in the fridge in an airtight container for about a week.

# Ganache Glaze

Ganache is a highly versatile, rich mixture of chocolate and cream that can be used as a frosting, a glaze, a sauce, to make truffles, or as a filling in cakes and pastries. The possibilities are endless.

**SERVING SIZE**

Enough to glaze a kg of chocolate sablé or to decorate a 24 cm (9.5 in) cake

1 recipe Whipped Chocolate Ganache (refer page 2)

**SERVING AND STORING SUGGESTIONS**

You can use ganache glaze for glazing tops of sablé or cakes or as a chocolate sauce on the side of a dessert like ice cream.

Once the ganache is done, it can last in the fridge in an airtight container for about a week and can be reheated in a water bath when needed.

Use the same ganache recipe as previous recipe on page 2, but do not set in the fridge to cool and do not whip.

Once the chocolate melts with the cream let it cool on the kitchen counter for about 10 minutes before using.

**TIPS AND TRICKS**

*If you want to make sure the glaze will harden (after you glaze tops of sablé or cake so that the chocolate doesn't melt or smudge), you can add a teaspoon of edible wax, if available, while melting the chocolate.*

# Graham Crackers

Did you know that the graham cracker was inspired by the preaching of Sylvester Graham, a devout Presbyterian Minister, who believed that minimizing pleasure and stimulation of all kinds, coupled with a vegetarian diet anchored by bread made from wheat coarsely ground at home, was how God intended people to live, and that following this natural law would keep people healthy? Interestingly, graham crackers are used in a variety of desserts today – from cheesecakes to muffins to pies.

## SERVING SIZE

Makes about 24 squares
For cheesecake: Enough for crust of one 20 cm (8 in) round cake

| | | |
|---|---|---|
| all-purpose flour | 300 g | 2½ cups |
| salt | 5 g | 1 tsp |
| baking powder | 10 g | 2 tsp |
| unsalted butter, cold and cut into pieces | 60 g | ¼ cup |
| honey | 80 ml | ¼ cup |
| molasses | 100 g | ⅓ cup |
| granulated white sugar | 60 g | ¼ cup |
| full cream milk | 60 ml | ¼ cup |
| vanilla extract | 3 ml | ½ tsp |
| cinnamon powder (optional) | 5 g | 1 tsp |

Preheat the oven to 180°C (356°F).

Prepare a baking tray, lined with parchment paper or greased with butter and dusted with flour.

Place your flour, salt and baking powder in the bowl of a hand-held electric mixer with the paddle attachment.

Add in the cold butter to the dry ingredients and beat on medium-slow speed until you get pea-sized pieces.

Add the honey, molasses and sugar.

Once incorporated, add the milk and vanilla.

Continue mixing until the dough is just formed.

Using your hand, take the dough out, shape it into a ball and place on parchment paper. Place another sheet of parchment paper on top of the dough.

Start to roll out the dough in a rectangular shape, about 35 cm × 20 cm and about ½ cm (14 × 8 × .2 in) thick.

Place it on a tray or cookie sheet and put it in the freezer for 10 minutes or fridge for 30 minutes.

*Continued >*

Once baked, the crackers
will last in an airtight
container at room
temperature for up to
2 weeks.

You can also wrap the
unbaked dough in cling
film and freeze for up to
1 month.

Remove from the freezer (or fridge) and score the dough with a knife or pizza-cutter horizontally and vertically to make square or diamond shapes.

Prick with a fork across the sheet to let air out of the dough.

Bake for around 20 minutes or until golden brown.

Once out of the oven, let it cool for about 10 minutes.

Then, using your hand or a knife, break through the lines you've scored to get the individual biscuits. It's important to do this while they are still soft because they will continue to harden as they cool down.

### TIPS AND TRICKS

*Make sure the butter you are using is cold and that the dough, once formed, also stays cold when you're working with it.*

*If, while you're working, the dough becomes too soft and sticky, you can always pop it back into the freezer for a few minutes.*

*If it's still sticky, add a little flour but make sure you add only a tablespoon at a time.*

*When you're rolling out the dough, keep in mind what you're using it for. We roll out the dough thinner when we want crisp biscuits for cheesecakes and toppings, and we make it thicker for gingerbread because we like it more chewy and cake-like.*

### VARIATIONS

- You can crumble them up in a food processor for puddings.
- Cut them out in squares for s'mores.

# Danish Biscuits

There are many varieties of butter cookies. One of the more popular ones is known as Brysselkex or Danish biscuits. These are unleavened cookies, often categorized as a 'crisp cookie' due to their texture, caused in part because of the quantity of butter and sugar.

## SERVING SIZE
Serves 6–8
Makes about a dozen biscuits

| | | |
|---|---|---|
| unsalted butter at room temperature | 80 g | ⅓ cup |
| powdered sugar | 40 g | ¼ cup |
| vanilla extract | 5 ml | 1 tsp |
| eggs | 50 g | 1 large |
| all-purpose flour | 130 g | 1 cup |

Preheat the oven to 160°C (320°F).

Prepare a baking tray lined with parchment paper.

In the bowl of an electric mixer fitted with the paddle attachment, beat together butter and sugar on medium speed for about 3 minutes or until light and fluffy.

Add vanilla and egg.

Gradually add flour and beat until well incorporated.

Transfer dough to a pastry bag fitted with a star or round tip.

Pipe 6 cm or 2½ in rings onto parchment-lined baking sheets, spaced 4 cm or 2 in apart.

Using the bottom of any round cup, dip the cup in flour and lightly press on each biscuit's surface to flatten them out to about 2 cm (about 1 in) thick.

Bake, rotating halfway through, for about 20 minutes until lightly golden around edges, but still light in color at the center.

Transfer sheets to wire racks; let cool completely.

### TIPS AND TRICKS

*When flattening the biscuits using cups, make sure you dip the surface of the cup in flour each time otherwise the dough will stick to the cup.*

*I like to use cups that have bottoms with designs and are not completely flat. That way the design imprints on the biscuits.*

*You can enjoy them as tea biscuits.*

## SERVING AND STORING SUGGESTIONS

The biscuits will last in an airtight container at room temperature for up to 2 weeks.

# How to flatten Danish biscuits

Pipe 6 cm or 2 ½ in rings onto parchment-lined baking sheets, spaced 4 cm or 2 in apart.

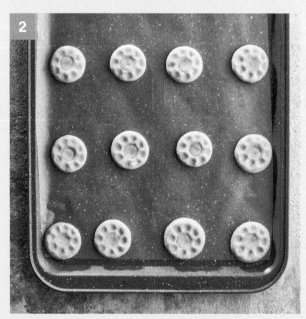

Using the bottom of any round cup, dip the cup in flour and lightly press on each biscuit's surface to flatten them out to about 2 cm (about 1 in) thick.

# Choux Pastry

According to some, a chef by the name of Pantarelli or Pantanelli invented the dough in 1540, 7 years after he left Florence with Catherine de' Medici and her court. He used the dough to make a gâteau and named it pâte-à-Pantanelli. Over time, the recipe of the dough evolved, and the name changed to pâte-à-popelin. Its irregular shape after baking earned it the name 'choux' (French for cabbage).

## SERVING SIZE

Makes about 30 choux bite-size pastries

| | | |
|---|---|---|
| vegetable oil | 125 ml | ¾ cup |
| water | 250 ml | 1 cup |
| granulated white sugar | 140 g | ⅔ cup |
| salt | 2 g | pinch |
| all-purpose flour | 200 g | 1½ cups |
| eggs | 250 g | 5 large |
| vanilla extract | 10 ml | 2 tsp |
| unsalted butter | 130 g | ½ cup + 2 tbsp |

## SERVING AND STORING SUGGESTIONS

The choux will last in an airtight container at room temperature for 2–3 days.

You can also freeze them in airtight bags for up to 2 weeks.

Preheat the oven to 180°C (356°F).

Prepare a baking tray lined with parchment paper.

In a deep saucepan, using a hand whisk, beat together the oil, water, sugar and salt on high heat.

Once the liquid starts to boil, lower heat and add the flour, using a spatula to fold the mixture together.

Continue folding until it starts to look/feel like a paste or pudding.

Remove from heat.

Put the mixture in the bowl of a hand-held electric mixer using the paddle attachment, and mix on medium speed. Keep mixing till it cools a bit.

Add in the eggs and vanilla and butter and mix until everything is well incorporated. Start spooning the dough with a teaspoon on the prepared baking tray, leaving about 2.5 cm (1 in) between 2 dollops.

Bake for about 20–30 minutes until the buns are crisp, light and a rich golden colour.

### TIPS AND TRICKS

*You can, alternatively, use a piping bag to pipe out the mixture into round dollops or whatever shape you would like, making sure you leave space between them on the baking tray.*

*If you are making éclairs, then you will need to use a piping bag to get the éclair shape.*

# Pastry Cream

Pastry cream, also called Creme Patissiere, is a rich, thick and creamy custard made from a mixture of milk, eggs, sugar, flour and corn starch (corn flour). Vanilla, liqueurs, chocolate, coffee and fruit purees are some complementary flavourings that can be added to the cream.

## SERVING SIZE
To fill 30 choux buns

| full cream milk | 500 ml | 2 ¼ cups |
|---|---|---|
| all-purpose flour | 30 g | 3 tbsp |
| corn flour | 30 g | 3 tbsp |
| granulated white sugar | 110 g | ½ cup |
| egg yolks | 100 g | 4 large |
| vanilla extract | 5 ml | 1 tsp |
| unsalted butter, cut in cubes | 140 g | ⅔ cup + 1 tbsp |

In a deep saucepan, bring the milk to a boil.

In a separate bowl, mix together the flour, corn flour, sugar, eggs and vanilla with a hand-whisk.

Once the milk boils, lower the heat and add the flour-egg mixture to the milk.

Continue mixing by hand until the mixture thickens. Remove from heat.

Add the butter and keep whisking until the butter melts in the mixture. It should be very shiny and pudding-like.

Have a bowl prepared with ice. Put another bowl on top of it and then place a sieve over it.

Push the mixture through the sieve with a rubber spatula. This will ensure you have a smooth cream with no lumps. The ice will cool it so the eggs don't get overcooked.

### TIPS AND TRICKS

*Add a vanilla bean to the mixture. The vanilla beans always add extra flavour and make the cream look more beautiful.*

*If the cream turns out lumpy, you can always blend it in a blender to smoothen it out. This is the fastest and easiest solution.*

*It is important to make pastry cream in a pot made of something other than aluminium or cast iron as they can discolour the final result, producing a greyish pastry cream that is not very appealing.*

### VARIATIONS

**Chocolate Pastry Cream:** Add 100 g (1 cup) of chopped bittersweet chocolate with the butter to the pastry cream and whisk by hand till the butter and chocolate melt.

### SERVING AND STORING SUGGESTIONS

You will use this cream when filling choux pastries or making other desserts.

The pastry cream will last in the fridge in an airtight container for up to 3 days.

# Simple Sugar Syrup

One of the simplest things to make, the humble sugar syrup is used to sweeten most Middle Eastern desserts.

## SERVING SIZE
Enough for two 24 cm (10 in) round trays of pastry or cake

| | | |
|---|---|---|
| water | 480 ml | 2 cups |
| white granulated sugar | 625 g | 2½ cups |
| vanilla sugar | 2 g | ½ tsp |
| lemon juice | 5 ml | 1 tsp |

In a medium-deep saucepan, bring water, sugar and vanilla sugar to a boil over high heat, stirring occasionally.

Once boiling, add the lemon juice and lower the heat.

Continue stirring every couple of minutes for 10–15 minutes until the liquid starts to thicken and reduce.

Take off from the heat and set it aside to cool.

## TIPS AND TRICKS

*Always prepare the syrup first before starting on a recipe that calls for it, as it will need time to cool down before it can be used.*

## SERVING AND STORING SUGGESTIONS

The recipes that call for this syrup don't all necessarily need the entire syrup. You may want to make the syrup and store it in bottles or jars either at room temperature or in the refrigerator.

In most recipes, you will need to just cover the pastry or cake with the syrup and allow it to soak. If you add extra, you can always drain out the excess syrup and reserve to reuse later.

It will last for 3–4 months.

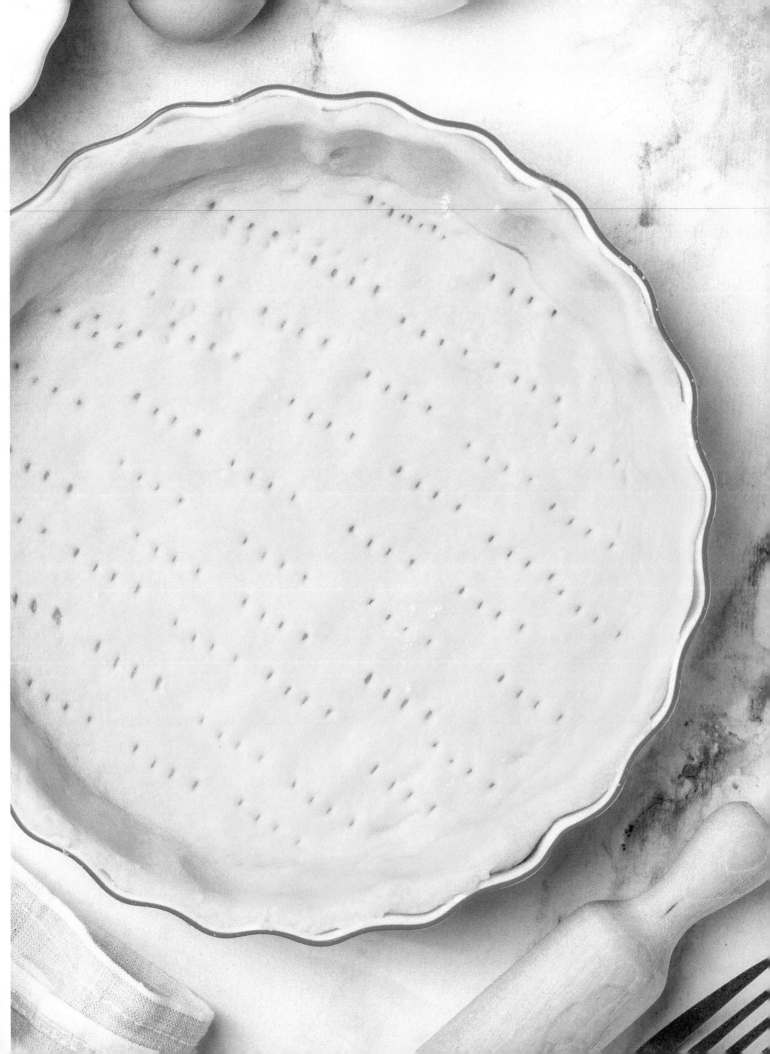

# Flaky Pie Crust

From being called the 'coffin' and the 'tiffin box', to being used to cage live birds inside as a surprise for guests, to being a delicate, butter-filled, tender casing, delightful on its own, the pie crust has come a long way. What used to be made from coarse flour in days past is now made of fine flour and creates a texture that complements the fillings inside.

**SERVING SIZE**

Serves 6–8

| all-purpose flour | 450 g | 3 ½ cups |
| --- | --- | --- |
| unsalted butter, cold | 300 g | 1 ½ cups |
| cold water | 135 ml | ⅔ cup |
| salt | 5 g | 1 tsp |

Prepare a 22 cm (9 in) tart pan by greasing the pan with butter.

In the bowl of a hand-held electric mixer with the paddle attachment, mix the flour and cold butter on medium-high speed until the butter becomes pea-sized.

Add salt to the cold water and then pour it on the flour-butter mixture. Continue mixing until the dough comes together into a ball.

Divide the ball into two round disks, cover each separately in cling film and place in the fridge for at least 1 hour or overnight.

When ready to work with the dough, place a large piece of parchment paper on the work surface, place the dough on it and cover with another piece of parchment paper.

Using a rolling pin, roll out the dough to about a 30 cm (12 in) round shape.

Remove the top parchment paper and use a fork to poke the base all over, making holes so that the dough doesn't puff up while in the oven.

Cover the dough with the parchment paper and chill for another 30 minutes.

Remove and place on tart pan lined with parchment paper.

Depending on what you need the crust for, you can bake at 180°C (356°F) for about 25–30 minutes until golden brown, or follow the instructions of the recipe it's being used for.

**TIPS AND TRICKS**

*When the dough comes together, you will still be able to see pieces of butter. That's ok, as it should not be completely smooth.*

*Always make sure you are working with cold dough to ensure a flaky crust.*

**SERVING AND STORING SUGGESTIONS**

Unbaked dough will last wrapped in cling film for up to a month in the freezer.

# Basic Ladyfingers

The tradition associated with this one has definitely passed down generations in my family. My grandma would always have these biscuits in her pantry. She used them to whip up a trifle, layer up tiramisu or simply to have at tea time. Because my mom loved chocolate, grandma would make a few extra with cocoa powder for my mom to dip in milk.

Now when I make them, I have to leave aside a couple for my kids to have with milk as well!

## SERVING SIZE
Makes about 24 ladyfingers

| | | |
|---|---|---|
| eggs, yolks and whites separated | 300 g | 6 large |
| vanilla extract or powder | 10 g | 2 tsp |
| white granulated sugar | 150 g | ¾ cup |
| all-purpose flour | 165 g | 1¼ cups |
| powdered sugar | 130 g | 1 cup |

## VARIATIONS
You can add 1 tablespoon of cocoa powder (10 g) to the egg yolk mixture to make a chocolate variation.

### SERVING AND STORING SUGGESTIONS
Once cooled, remove from parchment paper.

They will last in an airtight container for up to a month at room temperature.

Preheat the oven to 180°C (356°F).

Prepare a baking sheet lined with parchment paper.

Prepare a large pastry bag with a 1 cm (½ in) tip and set aside.

Lay out 2 sheets of parchment paper and draw the shapes of the ladyfingers you want. Make sure each drawing is at least 2 cm (1 in) apart.

Using the bowl of a hand-held electric mixer fitted with the whisk attachment, whisk the egg whites and 1 teaspoon of the vanilla until frothy. While whisking, gradually add half the sugar. Beat for 1–2 minutes, or until stiff peaks form (refer to page xi).

Gently, with a spatula, move the egg whites to a separate bowl.

Fold in the flour slowly using the spatula and set aside.

Using the same bowl and whisk (no need to wash equipment), whisk the yolks, vanilla and the remaining half of the sugar on high speed for 1–2 minutes or until the mixture is thick and pale.

Fold ⅓ of the whites into the yolk mixture, then gently fold in the remaining whites until just incorporated.

Using a spatula, fill the pastry bag with the batter.

Pipe the ladyfingers onto the shapes you drew on the parchment paper.

Using a sifter, sprinkle the ladyfingers with confectioners' sugar and make sure all of them are completely covered (the sugar will fall all over the parchment paper, and that's ok).

Bake for about 20 minutes or until golden.

Transfer to a wire rack to cool.

### TIPS AND TRICKS
*If you don't have a pastry bag or tips you can use a plastic sandwich bag or ziploc; put the dough in and when ready to pipe just cut the tip with scissors. Be careful. Once you cut the tip, the dough will pour out, so hold it tilted to the side when you are moving from piping 1 ladyfinger to another.*

# Sponge Cake

Sponge cakes are usually light cakes that are able to hold themselves really well. Because they can endure many layers on top of each other without collapsing, and as they can easily be moulded into all kinds of shapes, sponge cakes are usually a go-to for occasion cakes. The cake itself is dry and needs to be sprinkled in syrup or juice sometimes to make it moist. Usually sponge cakes don't have much flavour and rely on fillings and topping to build the required character of the final cake.

## SERVING SIZE

Serves 10–12

| | | |
|---|---|---|
| eggs | 500 g | 10 large |
| salt | 1 g | pinch |
| vanilla extract | 10 ml | 2 tsp |
| powdered sugar | 250 g | 2 cups |
| all-purpose flour | 250 g | 2 cups |
| baking powder | 5 g | 1 tsp |

Preheat the oven to 180°C (356°F).

Prepare a 28 cm (11 in) cake pan greased with butter and dust with flour.

Sift together flour and baking powder and set aside.

In a hand-held electric mixer with the whisk attachment, beat the eggs, salt and vanilla on high speed for about 5 minutes, until the eggs are pale yellow and have tripled in volume.

Add the sugar and continue to beat for another minute.

Take the bowl out of the mixer and using a rubber spatula, slowly fold in the flour and baking powder.

Pour in the prepared tray and bake for about 40–45 minutes. The cake is ready when the top springs back up when touched.

Fill and decorate the cake according to the recipe you are following.

### TIPS AND TRICKS

*It is much easier to bake the cakes in baking sheets so that you don't have to split them to fill them. Using the baking sheets, you can just fill and assemble right away. They will even bake faster since they are much thinner.*

### SERVING AND STORING SUGGESTIONS

You will use this cake as directed in different recipes, but this base will last up to 2 days wrapped in cling film at room temperature or in the freezer for up to a month.

### VARIATIONS

For a chocolate sponge cake, replace 50 grams (½ cup) flour with 50 g (½ cup) cocoa powder.

# Chiffon Cake

The recipe of the versatile Chiffon cake is credited to Harry Baker (1883–1974), a Californian insurance salesman turned caterer. Baker kept the recipe secret for 20 years, until he sold it to General Mills, which spread the recipe through marketing materials in the 1940s and 1950s under the name 'chiffon cake', and a set of 14 recipes and variations was released to the public in a Betty Crocker pamphlet published in 1948.

## SERVING SIZE
Serves 10–12

| all-purpose flour | 270 g | 2 cups + 1 tbsp |
| --- | --- | --- |
| powdered sugar | 160 g | 1¼ cups |
| baking powder | 10 g | 2 tsp |
| salt | 1 g | pinch |
| vegetable oil | 110 g | ¾ cup |
| egg yolks | 130 g | ⅔ cup |
| water | 175 ml | 1 cup |
| vanilla extract | 10 ml | 2 tsp |
| lemon zest | 5 g | 1 tsp |
| egg white | 300 g | 1 cup |
| cream of tartar or lemon juice | 5 g | 1 tsp |

Preheat the oven to 180°C (356°F).

Prepare a 28 cm (11 in) round cake pan by greasing it with oil and dusting with flour.

Sift flour, sugar and baking powder twice into a bowl. Add the salt and set aside.

In a separate bowl, whisk the oil, egg yolks, water, vanilla and lemon zest by hand.

Make a well in the middle of the flour mixture and add the yolk mixture and whisk briskly by using a hand whisk until everything is incorporated.

Using a hand-held electric mixer with the whisk attachment, whisk the egg whites on medium speed for a couple of minutes until frothy.

Add the cream of tartar (or lemon juice) and continue to beat until the egg whites start to hold stiff peaks (refer to page xi).

Using a rubber spatula, fold in the whites into the yolk mixture, bit by bit, making sure to fold it in very gently.

Pour the mixture into the prepared pan and bake until a knife or toothpick comes out clean at the centre. It will bake in about 45 minutes to an hour.

Let it cool completely before dividing the cake (follow directions given on page xiii for dividing cakes).

Fill and decorate the cake according to the recipe you are following.

## SERVING AND STORING SUGGESTIONS

You will use this cake as directed in different recipes, but this base will last up to 2 days wrapped in cling film at room temperature or in the freezer for up to a month.

## TIPS AND TRICKS

*It is much easier to bake the cakes in baking sheets so that you don't have to split them to fill them. Using the baking sheets, you can just fill and assemble right away. They will even bake faster since they are much thinner.*

## VARIATIONS

For a chocolate chiffon cake, replace 50 g (⅓ cup) of flour with cocoa powder.

# Apricot Jam

Jams are a product part of the sweet fruit preserves family and have a variety of applications or uses. Jams are made of whole fruit cut into pieces or crushed, then heated with water and sugar until they reach the 'jelling' or 'setting' point. This is achieved through the action of natural or added pectin, after which the jam is sealed in containers to make it last.

## SERVING SIZE

Yields 4 large 450 g jars

| | | |
|---|---|---|
| white granulated sugar | 2.5 kg | 12 cups |
| very ripe apricots, pitted and halved | 3 kg | 12 cups |
| water | 150 ml | ⅔ cup |

## SERVING AND STORING SUGGESTIONS

Store the jam in the refrigerator.

It will last up to a year.

Preheat the oven to 200°C (392°F) for about 20 minutes.

Sterilise four 450 g (16 oz) glass jars (see instructions below).

Spread the sugar in a large baking tray.

Turn off the oven and place the sugar in the hot oven for about 15–20 minutes, stirring occasionally.

Place the apricots and water in a large, deep pot over low heat.

Cook for about 15 minutes until the apricots start to become tender.

When they do, add the warmed sugar and continue to cook for about an hour, until it simmers.

The texture should start to become jam-like. You will know it's ready when you tilt a spoonful and it falls in sheets from the spoon.

Remove from heat, spoon out any foam from the top and discard it.

Pour the jam into prepared jars and allow it to cool completely before covering with the lids and refrigerating.

### TIPS AND TRICKS

*To sterilise the jars:*
- *First wash them thoroughly. Make sure you rinse out the soap very well. Fill a large, deep pot with hot water and bring to a boil on high heat for about 10 minutes.*
- *Discard the water. This sterilises the pot.*
- *Repeat the process, this time putting in the jars and lids to sterilize them.*

*Once done, dry the jars and lids very well with disposable kitchen towels.*

# Raspberry Jam

| fresh or frozen raspberries | 2.2 kg | 22 cups |
|---|---|---|
| granulated white sugar | 1 kg | 5 cups |
| lemon juice | 20 ml | 2 tbsp |

Sterilise four 450 g (16 oz) glass jars (see instructions below).

Place the raspberries and the sugar in a large, deep saucepan and bring to a boil over medium heat.

Reduce the heat and simmer, stirring occasionally, for about 45–60 minutes or until most of the liquid has evaporated.

Remove from heat and add the lemon juice, spooning out and discarding any foam from the top.

Pour the jam into prepared jars.

Allow it to cool completely before covering with the lids and refrigerating.

Cover and place in the refrigerator.

### TIPS AND TRICKS

*To sterilise the jars:*

- *First wash them thoroughly. Make sure you rinse out the soap very well. Fill a large, deep pot with hot water and bring to a boil on high heat for about 10 minutes.*
- *Discard the water. This sterilises the pot.*
- *Repeat the process, this time putting in the jars and lids to sterilise them. This is very important in order to remove all the bacteria so that the jam doesn't go bad.*

*Once done, dry the jars and lids very well with disposable kitchen towels.*

*Make sure you are continuously stirring so that the fruit and sugar don't burn.*

### VARIATIONS

Substitute strawberries for the raspberries to make strawberry jam.

### SERVING AND STORING SUGGESTIONS

The jam needs to be stored in the refrigerator.

It will last for up to a year.

# Tomato Jam

**SERVING SIZE**

Yields 4 large 450 g jars

| ripe sweet tomatoes | 5 kg | 25 cups |
|---|---|---|
| granulated white sugar | 1.6 kg | 8 cups |
| lemon juice | 65 ml | ¼ cup |
| nutmeg | 10 g | 2 tsp |

Sterilise four 450 g (16 oz) glass jars (see instructions below).

Fill a large pot with water and bring to a boil.

Add the tomatoes, a bunch at a time. Let them sit in boiling water for just a minute and remove right away, placing in a separate bowl filled with cold water.

Remove the tomatoes from the cold water and peel the skins off.

Put the peeled tomatoes back in a large, empty pot and add sugar, lemon juice and nutmeg.

Bring this tomato mixture to a boil over high heat.

Once the tomatoes release all their juice and start to boil, reduce heat and continue to cook for about 45–60 minutes, stirring continuously, until the puree thickens and no longer seems watery.

Spoon any foam from the top and discard it. Place the jam in sterilised glass jars and let them cool completely before covering and refrigerating.

**TIPS AND TRICKS**

*To sterilise the jars:*
- *First wash them thoroughly. Make sure you rinse out the soap very well. Fill a large, deep pot with hot water and bring to a boil on high heat for about 10 minutes.*
- *Discard the water. This sterilises the pot.*
- *Repeat the process, this time putting in the jars and lids to sterilise them. This is very important in order to remove all the bacteria so that the jam doesn't go bad.*

*Once done, dry the jars and lids very well with disposable kitchen towels.*

*Make sure you are continuously stirring so that the fruit and sugar don't burn.*

**SERVING AND STORING SUGGESTIONS**

Make sure the jars are properly sealed.

The jam needs to be stored in the refrigerator.

It will last up to a year.

# Winter

Winter visits differently in various parts of the Middle East, depending on where one is from. And with each shade of winter comes intensely personal experiences and habits. The intensity of the deep flavours of winter – ranging from cinnamon to nutmeg to cloves – tantalises taste buds and elevates simple desserts into delicacies.

It's the perfect combination – sweet delights, sometimes with tea, sometimes with coffee, bringing warmth to cold hands and noses. And who doesn't like something straight out of the oven – warm, inviting and cosy on a wintry night?

My mother lived in the city of Alexandria. Winters were extra cold and gloomy by the sea. They often had rain and storms and would stay home to warm up while baking.

Mother reminisces about winters in grandma's kitchen. Winters, she remembers, were always a busy time for baking a mix of international desserts and traditional Middle Eastern delicacies. One reason, of course, was to banish winter blues. The other, main reason was their neighbours. The building was mostly inhabited by foreigners who celebrated Christmas. Grandma would regularly bake and pack fresh Christmas goodies as gifts for her neighbours and their children. Of course, mother chuckles, they enjoyed the 'samples' of all those delicious gifts!

She fondly remembers, with closed eyes, almost as though inhaling the fragrances again, the kitchen oven warming up the house and the smell of cinnamon and other winter spices hitting her nose as she walked in after a long day at school.

All winter, as these recipes show, grandma would bake up a storm of decadent desserts that would make winter days something to look forward to. I too have seen my own children rush to their grandmother, my mother, as she bakes some of the recipes from this section. The fragrance of grandmother's love becomes entwined with the aroma of whatever is baking in that oven …

Happy winters!

# Chocolate Souffle

While the earliest mention of the soufflé is attributed to French master cook Vincent La Chapelle, in the early eighteenth century, the development of the soufflé, as we know it today, is usually traced to French chef Marie-Antoine Carême in the early nineteenth century. The word soufflé is of the French verb souffler, which means 'to blow', 'to breathe', 'to inflate' or 'to puff'.

**SERVING SIZE**

6–8 servings

| | | |
|---|---|---|
| bittersweet chocolate, chopped in small pieces | 375 g | 2 cups |
| unsalted butter | 125 g | 1 cup |
| egg yolks | 175 g | 7 |
| egg whites | 200 g | 8 |
| white granulated sugar | 87.5 g | ⅓ cup |

Preheat the oven to 190°C (374°F).

Prepare a deep, 24 cm (10 in) wide round Pyrex dish or around 6–7 small ramekins. Using a silicon brush, brush the Pyrex or ramekins (base and sides) with melted butter. Sprinkle with granulated sugar and tap out any extra sugar.

In a medium saucepan, melt butter on medium heat, making sure it doesn't start to burn or change colour.

Once melted, remove from heat.

Add chopped chocolate to melted butter.

Let the chocolate sit for a minute then mix with a rubber spatula or wooden spoon until the chocolate, too, melts, sit a side.

Using a hand-held electric mixer with a whisk attachment, beat the egg yolks and half the sugar on high speed for 2–3 minutes or until the mixture is light in colour – very pale yellow, with a lot of air bubbles.

Gently move the yolk to another large bowl.

Wash and dry the bowl and whisk handle very well.

In the cleaned electric mixer bowl using the whisk attachment, beat the egg whites and the remaining half of the sugar on high speed until it reaches white fluffy (stiff) peaks (refer to page xi).

Meanwhile, add the chocolate mix to egg yolks and sugar, folding it in with a rubber spatula or wooden spoon.

Slowly, using a rubber spatula, add the egg-whites to the yolk and chocolate mix, bit by bit, going all the way into the bowl and folding in the egg whites until completely incorporated. Be extra gentle at this stage.

*Continued >*

Serve with a scoop of vanilla ice cream or a dollop of fresh cream on the side.

Once baked, the souffle has to be eaten right away. However, you can prepare it in advance.

Cover the top well with cling film and refrigerate it for up to a week. Take it out of the fridge about an hour prior to baking.

Make sure it's at room temperature before you bake it so that it bakes evenly; otherwise you might get a souffle that is puffed up, but with a centre that is cold and uncooked.

Pour into the ramekins/plate, leaving around 3 cm (1 in) from the top of the bowl. If it is filled all the way to the top, the souffle will overflow.

Gently place them on a baking tray and bake for 10–15 minutes for little ramekins or around 40–45 minutes for a large Pyrex. As a general rule, your souffle will be ready once it's puffed up. Leave it an extra 5 minutes to set, and not any longer, so you don't have an over-baked souffle.

Take out of the oven and very gently place on the counter so all the fluffiness does not collapse.

Let it set for 5–10 minutes and serve right away while hot.

### TIPS AND TRICKS

*When you are making the chocolate-egg mix, move your rubber spatula from all the way at the bottom of the bowl to the top in order to properly mix until the mixture is all covered in chocolate. Make sure you are working delicately.*

*Always make sure the sugar is very clean and has no butter or other ingredients mixed with it as it could ruin the soufflé.*

*You* **must** *leave room in the dish for the souffle to fluff up. Also, be careful when you are handling the bowls, as any aggressive movement will force the air bubbles out and it might not fluff up.*

*If the souffle collapses (doesn't stay fluffed up), it's never a big deal. It will still taste just as good. You can always hide the top with powdered sugar!*

# Gingerbread Cookies

Thank Queen Elizabeth I for adorable little gingerbread people. While she didn't actually bake the cookies herself (she was a queen, after all), she did request that her royal bakers create gingerbread cookies shaped like visiting dignitaries in order to honour them. Ginger, with all of its health benefits, will not only protect you from getting a cold during the winter but, in gingerbread cookie form, will also help keep you happy and cosy with a hot cup of coffee.

**SERVING SIZE**

Makes 24 cookies

| | | |
|---|---|---|
| all-purpose flour | 300 g | 2 ¼ cups |
| salt | 5 g | 1 tsp |
| baking powder | 10 g | 2 tsp |
| ginger powder | 5 g | 1 tsp |
| ground cloves | 2 g | ½ tsp |
| ground black pepper | 5 g | 1 tsp |
| ground nutmeg | 2 g | ½ tsp |
| cinnamon powder (optional) | 5 g | 1 tsp |
| unsalted butter, cold and cut into pieces | 60 g | ¼ cup |
| honey | 60 ml | ¼ cup |
| molasses | 100 g | ⅓ cup |
| white granulated sugar | 60 g | ¼ cup |
| full-cream milk | 60 ml | ¼ cup + 1 tbsp |
| vanilla extract | 3 ml | ½ tsp |

**FOR THE GLAZE**

| | | |
|---|---|---|
| caster sugar | 40 g | 4 tbsp |
| water | 20 ml | 2 tbsp |

Preheat the oven to 180°C (356°F).

Prepare a baking tray brushed with butter and dusted with flour or lined with parchment paper.

Place the flour, salt, baking powder and spices in the bowl of a hand-held electric mixer with the paddle attachment.

Add in the cold butter to the dry ingredients and beat on medium-slow speed until you get pea-sized pieces.

Add the honey, molasses and sugar.

Once incorporated, add the milk and vanilla.

Continue mixing until the dough is just formed.

Roll the dough out in a rectangular shape, about 35 cm × 20 cm (14 in x 8 in) between 2 sheets of parchment paper until it is about ½ cm (0.2 in) thick (for desired thickness – see variations).

Place it on a tray or cookie sheet and put it in the freezer for 10 minutes or fridge for 30 minutes.

Prepare the cookie cutters you would like to use.

Remove the dough from the freezer (or fridge) and start cutting it into the desired shapes.

Place the shapes on a baking tray lined with parchment paper, keeping them about 1 cm (0.5 in) apart. You can reuse the remaining dough by forming it into a ball, rolling out again and cutting shapes. keep repeating these steps till you've used up all the dough.

Bake for around 20 minutes or until golden brown.

Once out of the oven, let them cool completely.

*Continued >*

Once baked, the cookies
will last in an airtight
container at room
temperature for up to
2 weeks.

You can also wrap the
unbaked dough in cling
film and freeze for up to
1 month.

While cooling, prepare the glaze. Mix the sugar and water in a
bowl and once the cookies are cooled, use a silicon brush to
brush the glaze on top.

Wait for the glaze to set before stacking the cookies in a box.

## TIPS AND TRICKS

*Make sure the butter you are using is cold and that the dough is
cold when you're working with it.*

*If, while you're working, the dough becomes too soft and
sticky, you can always pop it back in the freezer for a couple of
minutes.*

*If it's still sticky, add a little flour but make sure you add only a
tablespoon at a time so you don't add too much.*

*When you're rolling out the dough, keep in mind whether
you like it crisp or chewy. We roll out the dough thinner when
we want crisp cookies and we make it thicker to have the
gingerbread more chewy and cake-like.*

## VARIATIONS

Since this recipe doesn't call for any eggs, it is safe to try a
small piece to check if you would like to add more spices.

# Tarte Tatin

The tarte tatin, named after the Tatin sisters who invented it and served it in their hotel as its signature dish, is a pastry in which the fruit (usually apples) is caramelized in butter and sugar before the tart is baked.

## SERVING SIZE
Serves 6–8

## BASIC RECIPE USED

½ recipe of Flaky Pie Crust (refer to page 19) following the instructions until you need to chill the dough.

## FOR THE TOPPING

| | | |
|---|---|---|
| white granulated sugar | 260 g | 1 cup |
| cold water | 20 ml | 2 tbsp |
| lemon juice | 2.5 g | ½ tsp |
| 1 vanilla bean | | |
| unsalted butter, cut into small cubes | 60 g | 4 tbsp |
| red gala apples peeled, cored and sliced to quarters | 500 g | 4 |

### SERVING AND STORING SUGGESTIONS

While the tart is best enjoyed warm on the same day, it will last, covered, at room temperature for up to 2 days and can be slightly reheated.

Enjoy with a side of vanilla ice cream.

Prepare a 24 cm (10 in) round pan greasing with butter.

Prepare the pie crust.

### PREPARE THE APPLE TOPPING

In a small saucepan, mix the sugar, water, lemon juice and vanilla bean on high heat and bring to a boil.

Continue to cook until the mixture starts to thicken and darken in colour, becoming golden/amber.

Once the colour starts to darken, remove the pan from the heat right away and add the butter and mix until it's melted and all incorporated.

Pour the mixture onto the bottom of the prepared pie plate.

Start arranging the apples around the bottom of the pan as close to each other as possible to cover the entire base, starting from the outside and working your way inwards in a circle.

### TO FINISH

Preheat the oven to 180°C (356°F).

Remove the prepared pie crust from the fridge onto a flat working surface.

Carefully using the palm of your hands, pick up the pie crust and place on top of the arranged apples to completely cover the base.

Bake for about 25 minutes until golden and flaky.

Keep your serving platter ready, lined with parchment paper.

Flip the tart on the serving platter immediately after bringing it out of the oven.

Allow it to cool for 5–10 minutes before serving.

### TIPS AND TRICKS

*Make sure to turn out the pie while it's still warm so that the caramel doesn't harden at the bottom of the pan and stick.*

# Linzer Cookies

Did you know that the small cut-out in the centre of the top cookie of Linzer cookies, exposing the underlying jam, is known as Linzer Eyes? The Linzer cookie continues to be very commonly used in celebrating Christmas and other holidays.

**SERVING SIZE**

Makes 25 cookies

**BASIC RECIPE USED**

Raspberry Jam (refer to page 28)

| | | |
|---|---|---|
| all-purpose flour | 260 g | 2 cups |
| salt | 2.5 g | ½ tsp |
| cinnamon powder | 2.5 g | ½ tsp |
| ground cloves | 2.5 g | ½ tsp |
| ground nutmeg | 2.5 g | ½ tsp |
| baking powder | 2.5 g | ½ tsp |
| toasted almond flour (ground almonds) | 180 g | 1½ cups |
| toasted ground hazelnuts | 60 g | ⅓ cup |
| unsalted butter | 230 g | 1 cup |
| white granulated sugar, divided in 2 small bowls | 165 g (55g/ 110g) | ¾ cup + 1½ tbsp, divided (¼ cup and ½ cup) |
| egg yolks | 40 g | 2 |
| vanilla extract | 5 g | 1 tsp |
| powdered sugar (to decorate) | 50 g | ⅓ cup |

Preheat the oven to 180°C (356°F).

Prepare a baking tray brushed with butter and dusted with flour or lined with parchment paper.

In a bowl, sift together flour, salt, cinnamon, cloves, nutmeg and baking powder and mix.

Stir in ground almonds and hazelnuts and set aside.

In a hand-held electric mixer with the paddle attachment, cream the butter and half the sugar for around 3 minutes or until light and fluffy.

Add the rest of the sugar and mix until well combined.

Add egg yolks with the vanilla extract.

Turn speed down to low and add the flour-nut mix gradually until everything is well incorporated.

Take the dough out of the mixer.

Divide the dough into 3 parts, wrap each with plastic wrap and refrigerate for at least 3 hours or overnight.

Take out 1 piece of dough from the refrigerator at a time.

Place the dough between 2 sheets of parchment paper and roll it out until 0.5 cm (0.2 in) thick.

*Continued >*

If not filled with jam, the
cookies will last up to
2 weeks in an airtight
container at room
temperature. Once filled,
they will last 2 to 3 days.

Use any kind of big, rounded cookie cutter and cut out the dough into the desired shapes. Lay them on prepared baking sheets, 2 cm (1 in) apart.

Make a hole in half the cookies in the middle for when you put the jam.

Place on trays and place in the refrigerator for at least 1–2 hours until cookies become firm.

Bake cookies for 10–12 minutes or until edges become golden in colour.

Take out and place on a wire rack for 10 minutes or until they have cooled down.

Place a teaspoon of raspberry jam in the center of each lower half of the cookies.

Shower the top side of the cookies with powdered sugar.

Slowly place the top of each cookie on its corresponding lower half and close like cookie sandwiches.

### TIPS AND TRICKS

*Get whole almonds and hazelnuts and toast them in the oven until lightly browned or golden. Put them in a processor only after light roasting.*

*You can use a smaller round-shaped cookie cutter to make the hole. When making the smaller hole in the middle of the cookies, if you don't have smaller cookie cutters, you can use any small bottle cap you have.*

*Don't sprinkle with sugar unless ready to serve, otherwise the sugar gets dissolved.*

# How to assemble a Linzer cookie

Use any kind of big, rounded cookie cutter and cut out the dough into the desired shapes. Lay them on prepared baking sheets, 2 cm (1 in) apart.

Make a hole in half the cookies in the middle for when you put the jam.

Place a teaspoon of raspberry jam in the center of each lower half of the cookies.

Shower the top side of the cookies with powdered sugar.

# Hazelnut Biscotti

From the battle camps of ancient Roman legions to coffee cup sides at Starbucks, the biscotti has travelled a long way. 'Biscotti', plural for 'biscotto' literally means twice-baked – bis, in Latin, means twice, and cotto means baked.

Who doesn't love a good biscuit that can be dunked in coffee – or, like we do it, in good old Nutella?!

**SERVING SIZE**

15–20
Makes about 25 biscotti

| | | |
|---|---|---|
| roasted unsalted hazelnuts | 70 g | ½ cup |
| unsalted butter, at room temperature | 115 g | ½ cup |
| white granulated sugar | 150 g | ¾ cup |
| eggs | 50 g | 1 large |
| orange zest | 12 g | 1 |
| vanilla extract | 1 tsp | 5 ml |
| all-purpose flour | 300 g | 2¼ cups |
| baking powder | 5 g | 1 tsp |
| salt | 3 g | ½ tsp |

Preheat the oven to 180°C (356°F).

Line a baking tray with parchment paper.

Finely grind the roasted hazelnuts in a food processor, set a side.

Using a hand-held electric mixer with the paddle attachment, beat the butter on medium speed for about 2 minutes or until it is light and creamy.

Add the sugar and beat for another minute.

Add the eggs and beat until the mixture is smooth and the eggs are all incorporated.

Beat the orange zest and vanilla until just incorporated.

Add the flour, hazelnuts, baking powder and salt.

Mix on slow speed until just combined.

Lightly flour your surface.

Divide the dough in 2 and place on floured surface.

Shape into 2 rectangular logs about the length of your prepared baking sheet.

Set the logs on the baking sheet, spacing them about 5 cm (2 in) apart.

Bake until they are set and lightly browned. It takes about 25–30 minutes. When you take them out, don't turn the oven off, you will need it again!

Let them cool for about 5 minutes before slicing them about 4 cm (1.5 in) wide.

Return the cut rolls to the baking sheet and bake them again until they are golden. This step takes only about 5 minutes, so don't leave the kitchen while they are toasting. They can very easily burn if they stay an extra minute.

Remove from oven onto a wire rack and allow them to cool

*Continued >*

## SERVING AND STORING SUGGESTIONS

Pack in an airtight container at room temperature. They will last for about 2 weeks.

Serve with Nutella as a dip.

## TIPS AND TRICKS

*When the logs are out of the oven it is best to use a serrated knife and mark the surface first to make marks exactly where you want to cut, then slowly start going deeper in the log to cut completely. The serrated knife will also prevent the logs from breaking.*

# Chocolate Chip Cookies

Like the history of a lot of recipes, the stories about the chocolate chip cookie are many. The most popular one is that of Ruth Wakefield chopping up Nestle's Semi-Sweet Chocolate and adding the tiny bits to her dough because she ran out of Baker's chocolate. She thought the chocolate would melt and spread through the dough. It didn't. And a new recipe was born! Nestle, of course, had a field day and carries the recipe on its semi-sweet chocolate packaging even today, all in exchange for a lifetime's supply of chocolate for her.

## SERVING SIZE
Makes 24 cookies

| | | |
|---|---|---|
| unsalted butter, cold | 230 g | 1 cup |
| soft light brown sugar | 350 g | 2 cups |
| eggs | 100 g | 2 large |
| salt | 3 g | ½ tsp |
| vanilla extract or 1 vanilla bean | 5 ml | 1 tsp |
| all-purpose flour | 400 g | 3 cups |
| bicarbonate soda | 15 g | 2 ½ tsp |
| bittersweet chocolate, chopped | 240 g | 1½ cups |

Preheat the oven to 180°C (356°F).

Line a baking sheet with parchment paper and set aside.

Using a hand-held electric mixer with the paddle attachment, on high speed, beat together butter and sugar well.

Lower speed and add the eggs one at a time, then add the salt and vanilla.

Stay on slow speed and gradually add the flour and bicarbonate soda. Mix in the chocolate chips.

Using an ice cream scoop or with your hands, scoop out the dough and place on the prepared baking sheet, making sure the cookies are at least 2 cm (1 in) apart.

Place the tray in the freezer for 15–20 minutes.

Bake for about 10 mins or until golden brown on the sides and still soft at the centre.

Let the cookies cool for about 5 minutes before turning them out onto a serving platter.

*Continued >*

## SERVING AND STORING SUGGESTIONS

Of course, they are best served right out of the oven, so you can serve as-is or enjoy with milk.

You can also make ice cream sandwiches out of the cookies.

They will last up to 4 days in an airtight container.

You can reheat them (for a couple of minutes in the oven or 30 seconds in the microwave) before serving.

## TIPS AND TRICKS

*If you are using an ice cream scoop, dip it in flour so the dough doesn't stick; if you are using your hands, brush the palm of your hand in flour and try to scoop it out with your palms such that the dough makes the same shape it would with the ice cream scoop.*

*If you have a scale, you can also measure each scoop to make sure all the cookies are the same size. Generally, about 50 g per cookie is a good size.*

*I find using vanilla bean or pure vanilla extract makes a huge difference.*

*I also like to use half milk chocolate and half bittersweet chocolate.*

*Using chocolate blocks and chopping them up always make for chunkier cookies instead of using chocolate chips.*

# Fudge Brownies

Brownies, with many, many recipes today, can either be 'cake-style' or 'fudge-style'. Fudge brownies typically are chewy on the outside and gooey inside.

The best memory I have of my grandma baking these brownies is of us licking the spoon with the leftover raw batter. When the brownies came out of the oven, we rarely waited until they cooled down. We would devour them right away, fighting over the edges – those were the chewiest parts.

This recipe, from my grandmother's archive, is the perfect blend of fudgy, chewy and crisp on the edges, with the dense taste of the bittersweet chocolate. It never gets old.

## SERVING SIZE

Makes 12 brownies

| | | |
|---|---|---|
| unsalted butter | 150 g | ⅔ cup |
| bittersweet chocolate, chopped | 170 g | 1 cup |
| powdered sugar | 250 g | 2 cups |
| eggs | 150 g | 3 large |
| sea salt | 3 g | ½ tsp |
| all-purpose flour | 130 g | 1 cup |

## SERVING AND STORING SUGGESTIONS

You can store these in an airtight container for up to a week.

Preheat oven to 180°C (356°F).

Butter a 22 × 33 cm (9 × 13 in) pan and dust with flour, tapping out any extra flour.

Melt butter on medium heat.

When completely melted, remove from heat and add chocolate. Let it sit still for a minute.

Mix with a hand whisk, spatula or a wooden spoon until melted.

Add sugar and continue mixing.

Add the eggs and salt and mix well.

Fold in flour until well-incorporated and pour in the prepared tray.

Bake for about 20 minutes or until the top is flaky. Remove from oven onto a wire rack and sprinkle a little sea salt on the top, if you like.

Wait, until completely cooled, to cut into 12 even squares or as desired.

### TIPS AND TRICKS

*If the chocolate doesn't completely melt from the heat of the butter, put it back on low heat for no more than a minute, continuously stirring it.*

*While melting chocolate, make sure you are continuously mixing when the chocolate-butter mix is on the heat, so that the chocolate melts smoothly.*

*To make sure the brownies are fudgy, take them out as soon as they set and the top gets flaky, even if a toothpick or knife comes out with some dough sticking to it.*

# Crème Brûlée

Also known as Burned Cream, Burnt Cream or Trinity Cream, the Crème Brûlée has the distinction of holding a Guinness Record! In Feb. 2005, more than 35 of the Orlando (Fla.) Culinary Academy chefs and students assembled the world's largest Crème Brûlée for some 300 visitors. Admission was free, but samples of the dessert were sold for $5, with proceeds going toward scholarship funds for the Boys and Girls Clubs of Central Florida.

**SERVING SIZE**

Makes 4–5 individual ramekins

| heavy cream | 550 ml | 2 ½ cups |
|---|---|---|
| 1 vanilla bean | or 10 ml vanilla extract | or 2 tsp vanilla extract |
| eggs yolks | 200 g | 8 |
| white granulated sugar | 170 g (and 100 g on the side for the top) | ⅔ cup (and 10 tbsp on the side for the top) |

Prepare a deep saucepan with the cream and vanilla.

Put on low heat until it becomes hot but not boiling.

Prepare 2 separate bowls, 1 on top of the other. In the bottom one, put ice and place a sifter over the top one.

Using a hand whisk, mix together the egg yolks and sugar.

When the cream starts to simmer, add a little bit of the cream to the eggs and sugar and keep mixing.

Then add this egg mixture back to the heat and whisk while the heat is on.

Keep mixing until the mixture thickens up a lot. (Don't stop mixing or else the eggs might get cooked!)

After the mixture thickens, strain it through the sifter in the top bowl using a hand-whisk or a rubber spatula.

Remove the strainer and mix until everything is incorporated.

Pour in plates and leave to cool completely.

Put in the fridge until ready to serve.

**TO SERVE**

Spread 1 tablespoon (10 g) of sugar on the whole surface of each plate.

Light a fire torch on top of the surface, moving very fast all around the surface until the sugar starts to harden and become a golden colour. Some parts can even be burnt. Make sure the torch is not too close to the plate – there should be at least about 5 cm (2 in) distance.

*Continued >*

## SERVING AND STORING SUGGESTIONS

The crème brûlée will last in the fridge for up to 3 days.

Once the sugar is burnt, the dessert must be served right away.

## TIPS AND TRICKS

*Work fast, continuously mixing, to make sure you don't get a lumpy crème brûlée.*

*Don't put the sugar on top of the prepared plates unless you are about to burn it, otherwise it will dissolve.*

*I like using vanilla beans rather than extract, because the little black pods always add extra flavour.*

*This recipe needs a fire torch for the best results. If you don't have one, you can broil it in the oven but you will not get the same result.*

# Pumpkin Puree

Authentic pumpkin pie filling features freshly pureed pumpkin flavoured with the spices traditionally found in pumpkin pie: cloves, cinnamon, allspice and/or nutmeg.

**SERVING SIZE**

6–8

| | | |
|---|---|---|
| cleaned and peeled pumpkin cubes | 1 kg | 9 cups |
| granulated white sugar | 390 g | 1½ cups |

**FOR THE BÉCHAMEL SAUCE**

| | | |
|---|---|---|
| full cream milk | 225 ml | 1 cup |
| heavy cream | 120 ml | ½ cup |
| vanilla extract | 5 ml | 1 tsp |
| granulated white sugar | 20 g | 2 tbsp |
| unsalted butter | 30 g | 2 tbsp |
| all-purpose flour | 40 g | 4 tbsp |

Prepare a 28 × 23 cm (11 × 9 in) Pyrex dish.

In a large, deep saucepan, put the pumpkin cubes and sugar on medium heat, stirring continuously with a wooden spoon.

The pumpkin and sugar will start cooking, releasing a golden syrup.

Continue to stir occasionally for about 2 hours or until it is fully cooked.

The pumpkin should start to absorb the syrup, darken in colour (deep orange) and become mushed.

Pour the mushed pumpkin puree into the Pyrex dish.

## TO PREPARE THE BÉCHAMEL SAUCE

While preparing the bechamel sauce, start the oven to preheat on 180°C (356°F)

Heat the milk, cream, vanilla and sugar in a medium saucepan.

Melt the butter in a pot over medium heat.

Add the flour to the melted butter and continue to cook until the flour is absorbed. It should be paste-like.

Use a hand-whisk to beat in the milk mixture continuously until there are no lumps.

Add the separately beaten cream, vanilla and sugar to the béchamel sauce.

Continue to cook on medium heat until it thickens, making sure you are whisking continuously.

Once it thickens, remove from heat right away.

*Continued >*

You can prepare the dish
in advance, allow it to
cool, cover and place in
the fridge. Do not broil it in
the case of storing. It will
last up to 4 days. Before
serving, place in the oven
to broil. It is best enjoyed
warm out of the oven.

## TO FINISH

Pour the béchamel sauce over the pumpkin puree.

Bake for about 15 minutes or until it starts to bubble at the top.

Switch the oven to broil the top until it becomes slightly golden.

## TIPS AND TRICKS

*It is very important to stir the pureed pumpkin while it is cooking,
about every 15 minutes, to ensure the bottom doesn't burn.*

*Also, continue whisking when making the béchamel sauce so
that it is creamy and doesn't create any lumps.*

# Cinnamon Rolls

Roman spice traders introduced the Sri Lankan cinnamon to Europe. Much later, Sweden began using it in its pastries, developing the kanelbulle.

In Sweden and Finland, cinnamon rolls are traditionally enjoyed during a coffee break, or fika, which is a get-together with friends. In North America, it is commonly eaten for breakfast or dessert.

**THIS RECIPE HAS DIFFERENT PARTS THAT NEED TO BE ASSEMBLED TOGETHER. PLEASE USE THE INGREDIENTS LISTS BELOW FOR PREPARATION OF THE WHOLE DISH.**

### SERVING SIZE
Serves 12–15

### FOR BASIC YEAST DOUGH

| | | |
|---|---|---|
| eggs | 150 g | 3 large |
| salt | 2 g | ¼ tsp |
| buttermilk | 170 ml | ¾ cup |
| heavy cream | 20 ml | 2 tbsp |
| granulated white sugar | 65 g | ¼ cup |
| active dry yeast | 15 g | 1 pouch (3 tsp) |
| unsalted butter, melted | 45 g | 6 tbsp |
| all-purpose flour | 530 g | 4 cups |

### FOR THE FILLING

| | | |
|---|---|---|
| unsalted butter, melted | 25 ml | 3 tbsp |
| brown sugar | 160 g | ¾ cups |
| cinnamon powder | 5 g | 1 tsp |
| salt | 2 g | ¼ tsp |
| apple chopped in small cubes (optional) | 1 | ½ cup |

### FOR CARAMELIZED HONEY OR MAPLE GLAZE (GLAZE OPTION 1)

| | | |
|---|---|---|
| unsalted butter | 170 g | ⅔ cup |
| brown sugar | 220 g | 1¼ cups |
| heavy cream | 120 ml | ½ cup |
| salt | 2 g | ¼ tsp |
| vanilla extract | 5 ml | 1 tsp |
| orange zest (optional) | 5 g | 1 tsp |
| chopped pecans (optional) | 70 g | ½ cup |
| honey or maple syrup | 80 ml | ¼ cup |

### FOR CREAM CHEESE GLAZE (GLAZE OPTION 2)

| | | |
|---|---|---|
| cream cheese, room temperature | 110 g | ½ cup |
| vanilla extract | 5 g | ½ vanilla bean or 1 tsp extract |
| powdered sugar, sifted | 140 g | 1 cup |
| unsalted butter at room temperature | 60 g | ¼ cup |

*Continued >*

Place the eggs and salt in the bowl of a hand-held electric mixer with the whisk attachment and mix for 30 seconds on medium speed until eggs are beaten well.

Add in the buttermilk and mix for another minute.

Switch to the paddle attachment and on medium-slow speed, add the heavy cream, sugar, yeast and melted butter (make sure it's not hot).

Continue mixing until everything is well combined.

Switch to slow speed and add half of the flour and mix until just combined.

Add the remaining flour and mix for 5 minutes on medium-slow speed.

The dough should feel slightly sticky.

Brush a large bowl with a thin coat of butter and place the dough inside.

Cover the bowl in cling film and make sure it's completely covered tightly and place in a warm area. Let the dough double in size for around 2 hours. In the meanwhile, prepare the filling. If you will use the caramalized glaze, prepare that as well.

### TO MAKE THE FILLING

Mix all the ingredients for the filling together with a spoon.

### TO ASSEMBLE THE ROLL

Coat your rolling surface with a thin layer of flour. Roll out the dough in a 45 cm × 35 cm (18 × 14 in) rectangle.

Spread the filling on top of the dough, leaving a little less than 4 cm (1.5 in) of the edges to seal.

Starting with long edge nearest you, roll up the dough into a cylinder. Seal by gently pinching the seam with your fingers.

Mark gently to create 12 equal portions, then slice them.

Place the rolls at least 2 cm (1 in) apart in a baking pan brushed with butter. Or if using caramel glaze, pour ⅔rds of the glaze on the bottom of the pan that you will bake the rolls in. This makes a really nice caramelized base. The tray should fit the number of rolls you put (don't get a tray too big as when they rise again, they should be all tightly placed together).

*Continued >*

# How to assemble a cinnamon roll

Spread the filling on top of the dough, leaving a little less than 4 cm (1.5 in) of the edges to seal.

Starting with long edge nearest you, roll up the dough into a cylinder.

 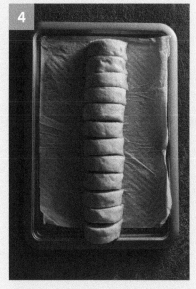 

Seal by gently pinching the seam with your fingers.

Mark gently to create 12 equal portions, then slice them.

Place the rolls at least 2 cm (1 in) apart in a baking pan

These will last for up
to 4 days in an airtight
container at room
temperature or in the
fridge. You can always
reheat them.

Tightly wrap the baking pan in cling film and let rise for
another 1½ hours. In the last 30 minutes, preheat your oven to
180°C (356°F).

Bake until puffy and golden around the edges.

Meanwhile, prepare your desired glaze.

### TO MAKE THE CARAMELISED HONEY OR MAPLE SYRUP GLAZE

Place all ingredients in a medium sized pot.

Cook over medium heat until very warm, but do not let it boil.

Pour over the buns once they are baked.

### TO MAKE THE CREAM CHEESE GLAZE

Using a hand-held electric mixer with the whisk attachment,
whisk together all of the ingredients.

### TO FINISH

Drizzle the desired glaze 10 minutes after removing the buns
from the oven.

### TIPS AND TRICKS

*To know if the dough is kneaded enough, put your finger in to
poke it. The dough should rise back up and should easily come
together in a ball when handled with lightly oiled hands.*

*I usually keep the oven on while I'm working and I turn it off
afterwards so it keeps the kitchen warm. This helps the dough
rise faster.*

# Chocolate Pudding

There are two main types of chocolate pudding: a boiled. then chilled dessert, texturally a custard set with starch, commonly eaten in the U.S., Canada, Germany, Sweden, Poland and East and South East Asia; and a steamed/baked version, texturally similar to cake, popular in the UK, Ireland, Australia, Germany and New Zealand.

Either way, chocolate pudding is chocolate pudding – an all-time favourite and an instant hit!

## SERVING SIZE
Makes 8 servings

| | | |
|---|---|---|
| full cream milk | 495 ml | 2¼ cups |
| heavy cream | 225 ml | 1 cup |
| corn starch | 40 g | ⅓ cup |
| white granulated sugar | 150 g | ½ cup |
| eggs | 150 g | 3 large |
| bittersweet chocolate | 50 g | ¼ cup |
| milk chocolate | 50 g | ¼ cup |

### SERVING AND STORING SUGGESTIONS

You can serve it warm (our family favourite) or refrigerate and serve cold.

If you refrigerate, do not reheat it. You can just leave it out of the fridge to get to room temperature in case you don't like it cold.

Serve it with a dollop of fresh cream and sprinkled graham cracker crumbs.

Chocolate pudding can be refrigerated for up to a week, but make sure it is covered well with cling film.

Prepare around 8 small ramekins.

Heat milk and cream in a saucepan. Bring to just under a boil.

In a separate bowl, combine the corn starch and sugar.

In a separate bowl or jug, whisk the eggs.

Add the eggs to the dry ingredients and whisk by hand until well-combined.

Slowly add half of the hot milk mixture to the egg mixture and make sure you are constantly whisking it so that the eggs don't cook!

Pour this mixture back into the saucepan (on low heat) with the rest of the milk and continuously whisk by hand until the mixture is thickened. This should take around 5 minutes.

Once thickened, pour the mixture through a sieve, using a spoon or spatula to push it through.

Add the chocolate and let it sit still for a minute or 2 before mixing it in. The heat of the pudding will melt the chocolate.

Use a blender or food processor to blend the mixture. Make sure there are no lumps. It should be silky smooth.

Divide the pudding in small ramekins and let them set. This should take around 30 minutes.

### TIPS AND TRICKS

*Don't worry if at any point the pudding is lumpy. Blending it at the end will make it smooth.*

# Spring

Spring – the time for birds to return from migration, for animals to awaken, for flowers to blossom and for the fragrances of honeysuckle and vine and all things citrusy.

Spring – also the time for picnics and yummy delicacies baked by mothers and grandmothers!

My mother's memories of spring are of lots of picnics in Alexandria. Alexandrian springs are the perfect time for picnics. The weather is fun, fresh and sunny with just the right temperature to be outdoors, running out barefoot on grass, with a gentle breeze flowing through your hair and just a hint of a drizzle. Yes, perfect, indeed!

With a twinkle in her eye, my mother recalls my grandma packing these beautiful rattan baskets with chequered picnic cloths for her and her friends. They used to be filled to the brim with a variety of goodies – from sandwiches to freshly baked biscuits and sweets.

Spring, she says, reminds her of those memories with her own mom even today through the taste of baked freshness, citrus, light treats and jams.

Spring was always a happy time that she spent in the beautiful Alexandrian weather. I find it to be the same with my children. I like to bake some of the treats that my grandma taught my mom and that she taught me and take both my mother and my children for picnics so they too can bond.

I hope the recipes that follow bring a smile to your face, stars to your eyes and, well, a spring in your step!

# Brioche

Brioche is of French origin – a pastry that crosses over with bread, but is made with milk, butter and eggs. The versatility of the brioche allows it to be sweet or savoury and it can be eaten for breakfast, lunch or dinner!

**SERVING SIZE**

Serves 10–12

**FOR THE DOUGH**

| | | |
|---|---|---|
| full cream milk, warmed | 280 ml | 1¼ cup |
| powdered sugar | 130 g | 1 cup |
| active dry yeast | 10 g | 2 tsp |
| all-purpose flour | 1 kg | 7¾ cup |
| eggs | 300 g | 6 large |
| vanilla extract | 10 ml | 2 tsp |
| unsalted butter | 180 g | ¾ cup |

**FOR THE EGG WASH**

| | | |
|---|---|---|
| egg | 50 g | 1 large |
| vanilla extract | 5 ml | 1 tsp |

**FOR THE TOPPING**

12 full boiled eggs, dyed whatever colour you choose

| | | |
|---|---|---|
| white granulated sugar | 130 g | ½ cup |

Brush a large bowl with butter and set aside.

In a small bowl, stir together warm milk, 1 teaspoon sugar and the yeast.

Let it stand for a couple of minutes until the yeast becomes foamy.

In the bowl of a hand-held electric mixer with the paddle attachment, add half the flour, the remaining sugar and the yeast mixture and mix on medium speed until combined.

Bring down speed to low and start adding the eggs 1 at a time.

Add the vanilla and continue mixing for about 2 minutes.

Stop the mixer and change the paddle attachment to a dough hook.

Continue mixing on medium-slow speed for another 5 minutes.

Gradually add butter and continue to mix until the dough is smooth and elastic. This should take about 10 minutes. If the dough is very sticky and watery, add flour, 1 tablespoon at a time. The dough is ready when you poke your finger in it and the dough bounces back up.

Make the dough into a ball shape and place it in the buttered bowl.

Cover it tightly in cling film and let rise at room temperature or in a warm area for about 1½ hours until it doubles in size.

Once it is ready, using your fist, gently punch the dough down.

Cover and refrigerate the dough for at least 1 hour or overnight.

Once ready to work with the dough, butter 2 baking trays and set aside.

Transfer the dough to a slightly floured work surface and divide the dough into 12 parts.

*Continued >*

The brioches will last in an airtight container at room temperature for up to 3 days without the boiled eggs.

They can be stored in the freezer for up to 2 weeks and reheated.

Roll each part into 3 individual ropes (25–30 cm/10–12 in).

Join the 3 ropes at the top, twist the ends one over the other as if braiding them and then join both ends to form a circle.

Place the braided rolls on the baking trays, making sure there is enough space between each one to allow them to rise.

Cover the baking trays in cling film and leave in a warm (or, at the very least, room temperature) room for another 1–2 hours until doubled in size.

At the last 30 minutes of the brioche proofing, start preheating the oven to 180°C (356°F).

Prepare the egg wash by whisking the egg and vanilla together in a small bowl.

Using a silicon brush, brush the tops of the brioches.

Sprinkle with the sugar.

Bake for around 20 minutes or until golden.

Transfer to a wire rack to cool and place your dyed egg in the center circle of each brioche.

### TIPS AND TRICKS

*To let the dough rise faster, you can preheat the oven while working so that the kitchen is warm.*

# How to assemble a brioche

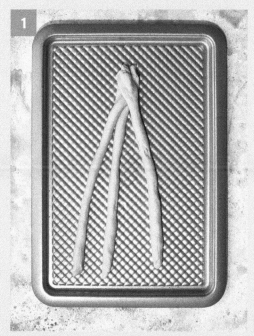

Join the 3 ropes at the top.

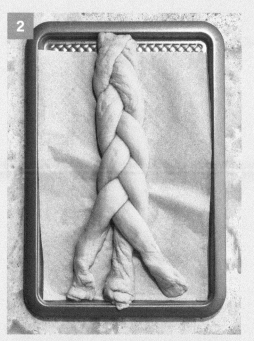

Twist the ends one over the other as if braiding them.

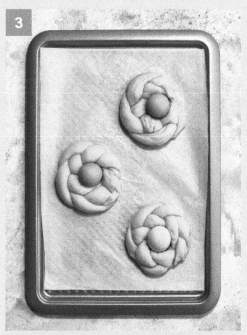

Then join both ends to form a circle.

# Fruit Tart (Sweet Tart Crust)

My mom says this was such a fresh and delicious treat that they would usually enjoy around teatime. The crisp crust with the cold and smooth vanilla pastry cream and fresh fruits on top, she remembers, was the perfect combination.

## SERVING SIZE
Serves 6–8

## FOR THE CRUST

| | | |
|---|---|---|
| unsalted butter | 350 g | 1½ cup |
| white granulated sugar | 325 g | 1¼ cup |
| egg | 50 g | 1 large |
| egg yolk | 20 g | 1 |
| lemon zest | 5 g | 1 tsp |
| vanilla extract | 5 ml | 1 tsp |
| all-purpose flour | 500 g | 3⅓ cups |

## FOR THE FILLING

1 recipe Vanilla Pastry Cream (refer to page 15)

| | | |
|---|---|---|
| halved strawberries (or any fruit of choice) | 500 g | 3 cups |
| apricot jam (refer to page 27) | 20 g | 2 tbsp |

Prepare a 20 cm (8 in) round, fluted pie tray by greasing it with melted butter and dusting with flour.

Using a hand-held electric mixer with the paddle attachment, beat butter and sugar on medium-high speed for 5 minutes until it becomes light and fluffy.

Lower speed to medium-low and add egg and yolk, lemon zest, vanilla and salt and beat another minute or two.

Bring mixer down to low speed and add the flour gradually until all is incorporated.

Make the dough into a ball, wrap in cling film and place in freezer for 10–15 minutes.

Meanwhile, make the pastry cream (refer to page 15).

Let it cool down and place in fridge.

Once cream is ready, preheat the oven to 180°C (356°F).

Take out the pie dough from the freezer and place it on a lightly floured surface.

Roll out dough using a rolling pin to about a 30 cm (12 in) round shape.

With the palm of your hands, pick up the rolled-out dough from the bottom and very carefully transfer to the prepared pie tray.

Gently press the dough into the edges of the tray.

Using a fork, poke the base all over, making holes so that the dough doesn't rise while in the oven.

Bake for about 20–30 minutes, until the edges start to crisp and become golden.

Continued >

If you used a tray with removable bottom, then remove the bottom and set the pie on a serving platter.

The tart will last, covered, in the refrigerator for up to 3 days.

Allow the tart to completely cool for 10–15 minutes.

Once the base tart is completely cooled, take out the pastry cream from the fridge and pour over the pie crust, making sure to evenly cover the entire base.

Start sorting the strawberry halves on top of the cream and brush the top with apricot jam for an extra shine.

## TIPS AND TRICKS

*If you have any excess dough around the edges, use scissors or a knife to cut it out. If the base has any cracks/tears, use the excess dough to cover it up.*

*If you didn't use a removable bottom tray, then leave it in the same tray to serve.*

*If the crust puffs up in the oven a little, don't worry about it. You will, anyway, be covering it with the cream and fruits.*

# Madeleine

The madeleine or petite madeleine is a traditional small cake from Commercy and Liverdun, two communes of the Lorraine region in North Eastern France. Madeleines are very small sponge cakes with a distinctive shell-like shape acquired from being baked in pans with shell-shaped depressions.

## SERVING SIZE

Makes about 40 bite-size cakes
Serves 8–10

| | | |
|---|---|---|
| unsalted butter | 270 g | 1¼ cups |
| white granulated sugar | 300 g | 1¼ cups |
| Zest of 2 large oranges | | |
| Juice of 1 orange | | |
| eggs | 300 g | 6 large |
| vanilla extract | 10 ml | 2 tsp |
| all-purpose flour | 270 g | 2 cups + 1 tbsp |
| baking powder | 8 g | 1½ tsp |

### SERVING AND STORING SUGGESTIONS

These will last for up to a week in an airtight container at room temperature.

Preheat oven to 180°C (356°F).

Prepare a silicon madeleine sheet.

Put butter and sugar together in a saucepan on medium heat and stir with a hand whisk.

Once the butter melts and the sugar is mixed well, turn heat off and keep mixing till it cools a bit.

Add the orange zest and juice to the sugar and butter mix.

Add eggs and vanilla and continue mixing.

Slowly add flour and baking powder and mix until just incorporated.

Pour the mixture into a jug, then pour into madeleine moulds.

Put in oven for 10–15 minutes.

Insert a toothpick into the cake. If it comes out clean, your cake is done.

### TIPS AND TRICKS

*If you don't have madeleine moulds, you can use mini cupcake moulds.*

*If you don't have a silicon sheet make sure to grease the molds with melted butter and dust with flour.*

# Crisp Meringues and Fresh Cream Platter

This was my grandma's go-to recipe when she didn't have time and had people coming over. She always said meringues needed to be chewy, like macaroons. Grandma served it with fresh cream and strawberries in winter or mangos in the summer. The recipe remains my mom's go-to as well when we are by the beach and she wants to whip up a quick dessert for us! She would always make a stock starting in springtime to prepare for Easter. She would fill large glass jars with meringues in pastel spring colours.

## SERVING SIZE
Makes about 80 small meringues

### FOR THE MERINGUE

| egg whites | 210 g | 7 large |
|---|---|---|
| salt | 1 g | pinch |
| vanilla extract | 10 ml | 2 tsp |
| powdered sugar | 520 g | 4 cups |
| cream of tartar or lemon juice | 5 g | 1 tsp |

### FOR THE CREAM FILLING

| heavy cream | 600 ml | 2½ cups |
|---|---|---|
| white granulated sugar | 30 g | 3 tbsp |
| 1 vanilla bean (optional) | | |

### FOR THE FRUIT TOPPING
500 g chopped strawberry or fresh mangos

Preheat the oven to 160°C (320°F).

Prepare a baking tray lined with parchment paper as well as a large, deep glass serving bowl.

In a hand-held electric mixer with the whisk attachment, beat the egg whites, salt and vanilla until frothy.

Continue beating on medium-high speed while adding sugar, a tablespoon at a time.

When stiff peaks form (refer to page xi) and it becomes glossy (after beating for around 5–8 minutes), add cream of tartar. Put the meringue in a piping bag with a star or round tip and pipe in small, round dollops directly on the prepared tray.

Bake for around 10–15 minutes until it sets in place and becomes hard on the outside.

Allow it to cool completely before using.

### TO MAKE THE WHIPPED CREAM

While the meringues cool: In the electric mixer, using the whisk attachment, beat the heavy cream, sugar and vanilla bean (if using) to firm peaks (refer to page xi).

Set aside.

*Continued >*

The meringue will last
up to 3 weeks in an
airtight container at room
temperature.

Once it is served with
cream, it is best enjoyed on
the same day.

## TO ASSEMBLE THE PLATTER

When the meringues cool, start by placing a handful of
meringue in the glass serving bowl, following by 4 tablespoons
of the chopped fruits, then 4 tablespoons of the cream.

Repeat with layers of meringue, fruit and cream until you fill up
the bowl.

The last layer should be covered with fruits at the top.

## TIPS AND TRICKS

*You can pipe the meringue in any shape you like.*

*You can make them slightly thick – about 3–4 cm (1–1.5 in) – to
make them chewier on the inside.*

## VARIATIONS

Once the meringue reaches stiff peaks, divide the meringue
in separate bowls and use different food colourings of choice.
Add a drop of colour, mix with a spoon, then add more colour
a drop at a time to reach the desired colour. Then continue
piping and baking.

Using pastel colours around Easter time make for very pretty
meringue decorations.

# Swiss Roll

A Swiss Roll is a rolled sponge cake with a filling, usually jam. In spite of the name 'Swiss roll', the cake is believed to have originated elsewhere in Central Europe, possibly Austria, in the 19th century. You slice it sideways across the end; each slice reveals a spiral pattern.

Did you know that the spiral layered shape of the Swiss roll has inspired usage as a descriptive term in other fields, such as optics, and especially the term jelly roll in science, quilting, etc.?

## SERVING SIZE
Serves 10–12

## BASIC RECIPE USED
1 recipe preferred jam (refer to Basic Recipes section, pages 27-29)

## FOR THE ROLL

| | | |
|---|---|---|
| all-purpose flour | 280 g | 2 cups + 2 tbsp |
| baking powder | 10 g | 2 tsp |
| eggs, separated | 300 g | 6 large |
| salt | 2 g | ½ tsp |
| white granulated sugar | 400 g | 2 cups |
| lemon zest | 5 g | 1 tsp |
| vanilla extract | 5 g | 1 tsp |
| hot water | 115 ml | ½ cup |
| unsalted butter, melted | 113 g | ½ cup |
| powdered sugar | 40 g | 4 tbsp |

## FOR THE FILLING

1 recipe preferred jam

| | | |
|---|---|---|
| heavy cream | 240 g | 1 cup |
| granulated white sugar | 20 g | 2 tbsp |
| 1 vanilla bean | or 5 ml vanilla extract | or 1 tsp vanilla extract |

Preheat the oven to 180°C (356°F).

Prepare a 30 × 43 cm (12 × 17 in) baking pan by lining it with parchment paper or brushing it with butter and dusting with flour.

Sift together the flour and baking powder, set aside.

In a hand-held electric mixer with the whisk attachment, beat together the egg whites and salt for 5 minutes or until stiff peaks form (refer to page xi).

Lower speed to slow and gradually start adding half of the granulated sugar.

Pour the egg whites into a clean bowl and set aside. In the same bowl of the electric mixer, beat the yolks with lemon zest and vanilla on medium-high for a couple of minutes until pale yellow in colour, with lots of air bubbles.

Lower the speed and gradually add the remaining granulated sugar.

Slowly add the hot water.

Add the melted butter to the egg yolks, continuously mixing so that the hot water and butter don't cook the eggs.

Once mixed well, add the egg whites to the yolk mixture and mix until just incorporated.

Stop the mixer and with a rubber spatula slowly add the flour, folding it in.

Pour the mixture into the prepared baking tray, making sure to spread the batter evenly into the prepared pan.

Bake for 10–12 minutes or until the top of the cake springs back when softly touched with your finger.

*Continued >*

**To make a chocolate Swiss Roll:**

- Add 3 tablespoons (30 g) of unsweetened cocoa powder with the flour, omitting the lemon zest.
- Optionally, you may add 1 tablespoon (10 g) instant coffee powder to the hot water.
- When turning over the cake, dust the parchment paper with cocoa powder instead of sugar.
- Follow the same instructions of filling the cake with the whipped cream and omit the jam.

**For the cake topping:**

- You will need 1 recipe Chocolate Ganache Glaze (refer to page 4).
- Make sure to place the cake on a wire rack with a baking sheet underneath it to catch the extra ganache that falls off the cake.
- Pour the ganache all over the cake, covering it entirely.
- Place it in the refrigerator for at least 30 minutes to allow the ganache to set before slicing it.

**SERVING AND STORING SUGGESTIONS**

Cut the cake into 4 cm (1.5 in) wide slices to serve.

It will last, covered, in the refrigerator for up to 3 days.

Once the cake is out of the oven, place a rectangular piece of parchment paper (larger than the cake) on a flat surface. Sift half of the powdered sugar covering the parchment paper.

Turn the cake onto the dusted surface and if you had baked it in parchment paper. Peel that sheet off.

Start to roll the cake tightly with the sugar-dusted parchment paper, starting with the edge closer to you (it should be the narrower edge). Make sure you are gentle so it doesn't crack.

Let it cool completely while rolled up.

**TO PREPARE YOUR FILLING**

Using a hand-held electric mixer with the whisk attachment, whip the heavy cream, sugar and vanilla extract on medium-high speed for about 2–3 minutes until stiff peaks form (refer to page xi).

Once the cake cools, unroll it very gently and remove the parchment paper.

Place the cake on a clean baking sheet.

Start to spread 4 tablespoons of jam evenly on top.

Using a knife or the back of a spoon, gently swirl the cream into the jam.

Slowly start to roll the cake back up.

Using a sieve, sprinkle the rest of the powdered sugar, making sure to cover the entire cake.

**TIPS AND TRICKS**

*When you pour the batter onto the tray, it should be a very thin layer.*

*Tap the pan on the counter to make sure the batter is evenly spread.*

*After rolling the cake in the parchment paper, it is very important to let it cool completely to room temperature before unrolling it, otherwise you may run the risk of the cake breaking apart.*

# How to assemble a Swiss roll

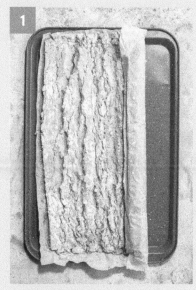

Place the cake on a clean baking sheet.

Start to spread 4 tablespoons of jam evenly on top.

Using a knife or the back of a spoon, gently swirl the cream into the jam.

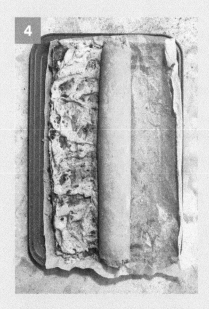

Slowly start to roll the cake back up.

Using a sieve, sprinkle the rest of the powdered sugar, making sure to cover the entire cake.

# Pasta Flora (a.k.a. Pastafrola)

Pastafrola is a type of sweet tart common to Argentina, Paraguay, Uruguay and Greece. It is a covered, jam-filled shortcrust pastry dish principally made from flour, sugar and egg. Italian immigrants brought it to Argentina and Uruguay. The dish is usually served as an afternoon dessert (merienda) or with mate (a South American drink), but may be eaten at any time of the day.

## SERVING SIZE
10–12

| | | |
|---|---|---|
| all-purpose flour | 500 g | 4 cups |
| baking powder | 5 g | 1 tsp |
| unsalted butter | 230 g | 1 cup |
| powdered sugar | 130 g | 1 cup |
| eggs | 100 g | 2 large |
| vanilla extract | 5 ml | 1 tsp |
| salt | 1 g | pinch |
| apricot jam (refer to page 27) | 400 g | 1¼ cup |
| yolk (for the egg wash) | 20 g | 1 |

## TIPS AND TRICKS

*When making the lattice pattern, don't worry about the pie edges looking good. Before serving you can lightly dust with powdered sugar to cover it up.*

## SERVING AND STORING SUGGESTIONS

It will last, covered, at room temperature for up to 3 days.

Prepare a 30 cm (12 in) round tart pan, by greasing it with butter and dusting it with flour or lining it with parchment paper.

Sift the flour and the baking powder into a bowl and set aside.

Using a hand-held electric mixer with the paddle attachment, beat the butter and sugar on high speed for about 5 minutes until light and fluffy.

Lower speed to medium and add the eggs one at a time, followed by the vanilla and salt.

Switch the speed to low and add the flour in 3 batches, until just incorporated.

Continue mixing on slow for a minute or 2 until the dough looks smooth.

Form the dough into a ball shape and covering with cling film, place in the refrigerator for at least 1 hour to set.

Remove from the fridge, cut off about ⅓rd of the dough and put it back in the fridge.

Preheat the oven to 180°C (356°F).

Place ⅔rds of the dough in the pan and using your fingers, spread the dough along the bottom and up the sides of the pan evenly.

Spread the jam over the dough, making sure it covers the entire base.

Take small pieces of the reserved ⅓rd dough and shape them into long, thin logs to go across the top of the crust.

Place the logs over the jam layer to form a lattice pattern.

In a small bowl, whisk the egg yolk with a drop of vanilla extract.

Brush the top of the latticed crust with a silicon brush.

Bake for about 35–40 minutes, until golden brown.

# Carrot Cake

The origins of carrot cake are disputed. Published in 1591, there is an English recipe for 'pudding in a Carret root' that is essentially a stuffed carrot with meat, but it includes many elements common to the modern dessert: shortening, cream, eggs, raisins, sweetener (dates and sugar), spices (clove and mace), scraped carrot and breadcrumbs (in place of flour). Many food historians believe carrot cake originated from such carrot puddings eaten by Europeans in the Middle Ages, when sugar and sweeteners were expensive and many people used carrots as a substitute for sugar.

**SERVING SIZE**

Serves 8–10

**FOR THE CAKE**

| | | |
|---|---|---|
| all-purpose flour | 300 g | 2⅓ cups |
| baking powder | 3 g | ½ tsp |
| baking soda | 3 g | ½ tsp |
| cinnamon powder | 10 g | 2 tsp |
| vegetable or sunflower oil | 325 g | 1½ cup |
| white granulated sugar | 500 g | 2 cups |
| eggs | 250 g | 5 large |
| vanilla | 6 g | 1 tsp |
| finely grated carrots | 225 g | |
| crushed walnuts (optional) | 50 g | ½ cup |

**FOR THE FROSTING**

| | | |
|---|---|---|
| unsalted butter, at room temperature | 90 g | 9 tbsp |
| powdered sugar, sifted | 520 g | 4 cups |
| cream cheese, at room temperature | 225 g | 1 cup |
| pure vanilla extract | 2 ml | ¼ tsp |

Preheat the oven at 160°C (320°F).

Prepare two round 24 cm (9 in) cake pans.

Brush your prepared pans with oil and dust with flour.

In a bowl, add together all the dry ingredients (flour, baking powder, baking soda, cinnamon) and set aside.

In a hand-held electric mixer with the whisk attachment, beat the oil, sugar, and eggs on high speed.

Add the vanilla.

Continue beating on high speed for about 5 minutes.

Lower the speed to slow and add the carrots.

Continue whisking for 2 minutes.

Stop the mixer and detach the mixing bowl. Slowly add the dry ingredients and mix by hand, using the palms of your hands going all the way in the bowl and out until all is combined. You can, alternately, use a spatula but make sure the flour is well incorporated.

Pour into the prepared pans, using your hand to keep tapping the mix to remove any large air pockets.

Bake for around an hour or until a toothpick comes out clean.

Let the cakes cool in the pans for 20–30 minutes.

Then run a knife around the edges of the cakes and turn them out onto a wire rack.

Turn the cakes right side up and allow them to completely cool.

*Continued >*

Serve right away or store until ready to serve at room temperature under a cake dome or in an airtight container to prevent it from drying out.

It will stay fresh for up to 3 days.

## MEANWHILE, PREPARE THE CREAM CHEESE FROSTING

Using a hand-held electric mixer fitted with the whisk attachment, beat the butter on high speed for around 3 minutes, until light and fluffy.

Then add the sugar and beat for another minute.

Add the cream cheese, a tablespoon at a time, until it is incorporated.

Add the vanilla extract and keep beating for about 5 minutes until it is fluffy.

Be sure to beat on high speed at the very end for at least 2 minutes to ensure that the frosting is light and fluffy.

## TO FINISH

Place one of the cake layers onto the cake platter you will be using so you don't have to move it around once it is assembled.

Spread a large dollop (5 tablespoons) of the frosting in the centre of the cake. Don't let it go to the edges.

Place a second cake layer on top and press lightly to allow the frosting to spread. Spread another dollop of frosting over the second cake and frost the top and sides of the cake, adding more frosting as needed.

## TIPS AND TRICKS

*Frosting cake is always much easier when the cakes are frozen. You can cover the cakes in cling film and freeze for a couple of hours or overnight. Take out the cake when ready to frost. This allows the cake to be firmer when working with it.*

*If you are making the frosting beforehand, you can keep it in an airtight container in the fridge for up to a week.*

*Before frosting the cake, let the frosting get to room temperature and beat it in the mixer for about 5 minutes to make sure it's fluffy.*

*You can also **crumb coat the cake**:*

- *Assemble the two layers together, cover with a thin layer of frosting and freeze. Remember, the cake gets crumbly when frosting it. Freezing it for a little while will make it stable and reduce how crumbly it is.*
- *Once the frosting is frozen, add a second frosting later to make sure the cake crumbs don't get mixed up with the frosting.*

# Sugar Cookies

The long history of manufacturing sugar cookies dates back to the 7th century in Persia. However, sugar cookies as they are known today were first made by Protestant settlers in the Nazareth colony in Pennsylvania in the 17th century. They were baked in the shape of the state symbol, a keystone. Sugar cookies are usually decorated with frosting, sugar icing and sprinkles before consumption.

## SERVING SIZE
Makes about 24 cookies

## FOR THE DOUGH

| | | |
|---|---|---|
| unsalted butter, cold | 350 g | 1½ cups |
| white granulated sugar | 150 g | ¾ cup |
| egg | 50 g | 1 large |
| vanilla extract | 5 ml | 1 tsp |
| salt | 1 g | pinch |
| all-purpose flour | 460 g | 3⅓ cups |

## TO DECORATE

| | | |
|---|---|---|
| powdered sugar | 450 g | 3½ cups |
| water | 160 g | ⅔ cup |
| meringue powder or egg white powder | 60 g | ⅔ cup |
| vanilla extract | 10 g | 2 tsp |
| Food colouring of choice | | |

Prepare a baking sheet, brushing it with butter and dusting with flour or lining it with parchment paper.

In a hand-held electric mixer with the paddle attachment, cream the butter and sugar on high speed until it is light and fluffy.

Add the egg, vanilla and salt and continue beating for another 2 minutes.

Scrape the bottom and sides of the bowl with a rubber spatula and beat for another minute.

Bring down the speed to low, gradually add the flour and continue mixing until just combined.

Form the dough into a ball, wrap in cling film and place in the refrigerator for at least 30 minutes to set.

Preheat the oven to 180°C (356°F).

Take out the dough from the fridge and divide it into 3 balls.

Dust a clean surface with flour, using a rolling pin also dusted with flour. Alternatively, place the dough between 2 sheets of parchment paper.

Roll out the dough into a rectangular shape about 0.5 cm (0.2 in) thick.

Using your preferred cookie cutters, cut the dough in desired shapes and place on a baking sheet, leaving 1 cm (0.5 in) space between each cookie. If you have excess dough, repeat the process of rolling out the dough and cutting cookies.

Bake for 10–15 minutes until golden.

Remove from oven and let cool completely.

*Continued >*

The cookies will last up
to 2 weeks in an airtight
container at room
temperature.

The icing will last in an
airtight container in the
fridge for up to 4 days.

## TO DECORATE THE COOKIES

In a hand-held electric mixer with the whisk attachment, mix together the sugar, water, meringue or egg white powder and vanilla on slow speed for about 5 minutes until smooth.

It should look like, and have the consistency of, glue. If you feel it is too thick, add a tablespoon of water, and if the icing is too thin add more sugar, a tablespoon at a time.

Divide the icing in separate small bowls and add the different food colourings of your choice, one drop at a time and mix with a spoon to see the final colour. Keep adding a drop at a time until you reach the desired shade.

You can use the back of a spoon or a knife to smoothen out the icing on the cooled cookies or use a piping bag to pipe out certain decorations or patterns that you would like.

Allow the icing to air dry on the cookies for about 10 minutes before storing away the cookies.

### TIPS AND TRICKS

*If the dough becomes warm while you're working it, place in the freezer for 10–15 minutes before placing in the oven. Baking cold dough makes for crispier cookies.*

*If you find that halfway through baking the cookies are turning golden from one side only, rotate the baking tray.*

### VARIATION

You can make **chocolate sugar cookies**. All you need to do is replace 30 g (¼ cup) flour with 50 g (½ cup) unsweetened cocoa powder.

# Profiteroles

Profiteroles, chou à la crème (both French) or cream puff (US), is a filled French choux pastry ball with a typically sweet and moist filling of whipped cream, custard, pastry cream, or ice cream.

**SERVING SIZE**

Serves 8–10

**BASIC RECIPES USED**

1 recipe Choux Pastry
(refer to page 13)
1 recipe Pastry Cream
(refer to page 15)
1 recipe warmed Ganache Glaze
(refer to page 4)

| | | |
|---|---|---|
| toasted almond flakes | 100 g | 1 cup |

**SERVING AND STORING SUGGESTIONS**

Serve right away. It is best enjoyed the same day.

The profiterole will last up to 2 days covered in the fridge.

Prepare a large, deep glass serving bowl.

Fill a pastry bag, fitted with any thin piping tip, with the pastry cream.

Using the piping tip, poke a hole in the bottom or side of each choux pastry and fill it with pastry cream.

Place all the filled choux buns in the large serving bowl and pour the warm ganache over it. Make sure you cover all the choux buns.

Sprinkle the toasted almond flakes on top.

**TIPS AND TRICKS**

*To warm the ganache glaze, put the ganache in a heatproof bowl and, using the double-boiler method, let it sit in a bowl of simmering water for about 5 minutes.*

**VARIATION**

**Ice cream profiteroles**

- Prepare 1 recipe of Vanilla Ice Cream (refer page 119).
- Scoop out 1 tablespoon of ice cream (enough for every choux pastry) on a tray lined with parchment paper and place in freezer for about 30 minutes.
- Meanwhile, halve each profiterole horizontally.
- Fill each half choux with the prepared ice cream scoops and place the other half on top to sandwich it.
- Place all the choux pastries in the prepared serving platter and follow the last two steps above to finish.

# Chocolate Birthday Cake

This has to be the best, ultimate cake for all chocolate lovers. This is a dense cake filled with bittersweet chocolate.

**SERVING SIZE**

Serves 8–10

**FOR THE CAKE**

| | | |
|---|---|---|
| all-purpose flour | 325 g | 2½ cups |
| unsweetened cocoa powder | 30 g | ¼ cup |
| baking powder | 15 g | 3 tsp |
| baking soda | 3 g | ¼ tsp |
| unsalted butter at room temperature | 225 g | 1 cup |
| powdered sugar | 290 g | 2¼ cups |
| eggs at room temperature | 300 g | 6 large |
| vanilla extract | 5 ml | 1 tsp |
| whole milk at room temperature | 225 ml | 1 cup |

**FOR THE FILLING AND TOPPING:**

1 recipe Whipped Chocolate Ganache (refer to page 2)
1 recipe Ganache Glaze (refer to page 4)

| | | |
|---|---|---|
| white granulated sugar | 70 g | ⅓ cup |
| crushed toasted hazelnuts | 200 g | 2 cups |

Preheat the oven to 180°C (356°F).

Prepare a 24 cm (9 in) round cake pan, brushed with butter and dusted with flour.

Sift the flour, cocoa powder, baking powder and baking soda in a bowl and set aside.

Using a hand-held electric mixer with the paddle attachment, beat the butter and sugar on high speed for 5 minutes, until fluffy.

Lower the speed to medium and gradually add the eggs one at a time.

Switch to slow speed, add vanilla, add the milk and slowly add the dry ingredients switching between the milk and dry ingredients until everything is incorporated.

Pour the mix in the prepared pan and bake for 10 minutes on 180°C (356°F). Then lower the heat to 150°C (302°F) for about 35 minutes.

Insert a toothpick. If it comes out clean, then the cake is ready.

Take out of the oven and allow it to completely cool.

## TO FILL THE CAKE

Once the cake is completely cooled, use a serrated knife to divide it in three layers (see General Tips on how to divide cakes on page xiii).

Place one cake layer on a cake stand, preferably the same diameter as the cake. Drop a large dollop (5 tablespoons) of whipped ganache on to the center of the cake layer don't let it go to the edges.

Place the second cake layer on top and press lightly to allow the ganache to spread. Repeat the process with the next layer of cake.

On the final cake layer, start covering the entire cake (top and sides) evenly with a thin layer of whipped ganache.

*Continued >*

It will last, covered, in the
fridge for up to 3 days.

If you are storing, don't put
the caramelized hazelnuts
in the fridge as they could
get soggy.

Decorate only right before
serving.

Freeze the cake for about 15 minutes.

Remove from the freezer and place on a wire rack. Make sure there is a baking tray under the wire rack.

Pour the ganache glaze on top of the cake, covering the entire surface.

Let it settle for a couple of minutes and allow all the excess glaze to fall off.

## TO DECORATE THE SIDES

Put the sugar in a saucepan on medium heat until it starts to turn gold.

Add the hazelnuts and make sure they are completely covered in sugar.

Leave on medium heat until the sugar starts to caramelise and becomes a deep golden colour.

Pour it on a silicon sheet or parchment paper to completely cool, then break it apart by hand or crush it to sandy texture by placing parchment paper on top of the hazlenuts and using a rolling pin to crush them.

Using the palms of your hands, scoop out the crushed caramelized hazelnuts and gently stick it to the sides, covering the entire cake.

## TIPS AND TRICKS

*It is always better to bake the cake a day before decorating it, as fresh cakes tend to be more crumbly.*

*While filling the cake layers, don't spread the ganache. Once you put the second cake layer, it will spread with the weight of the second layer.*

# Yellow Custard with Biscuits

Custard is a variety of culinary preparations based on sweetened milk, cheese or cream cooked with egg or egg yolk to thicken it, and sometimes also flour, corn starch or gelatine. Depending on the recipe, custard may vary in consistency from a thin pouring sauce (crème anglaise) to the thick pastry cream (crème pâtissière) used to fill éclairs.

**SERVING SIZE**
Serves 4–6

**BASIC RECIPE USED**
½ recipe Danish Biscuits
(refer to page 9)

| | | |
|---|---|---|
| full cream milk | 260 ml | 1 cup |
| heavy cream | 260 ml | 1 cup |
| vanilla extract | 8 ml | 1½ tsp |
| egg yolks | 80 g | 4 large |
| corn starch | 10 g | 1 tbsp |
| powdered sugar | 130 g | ½ cup |

**SERVING AND STORING SUGGESTIONS**

It is best served warm.

It will last in the fridge for up to 3 days.

If storing in the fridge, make sure to cover it with cling film, so the custard doesn't form a layer of skin. Don't reheat, you can still enjoy it cold or leave out to get to room temperature.

Prepare 6 ramekins or glass cups.

In a saucepan, put the milk, cream and vanilla on medium heat, stirring continuously until hot, but not boiling.

Remove from heat.

In a separate bowl, whisk egg yolks, corn flour and sugar until everything is combined.

Pour half of the hot milk mixture over the egg yolk mixture and continue whisking.

Pour everything back into the saucepan with the rest of the milk, stirring continuously, for 10–15 minutes until the custard thickens.

Remove from heat right away.

Pour the custard through a sieve in a clean bowl. Place this bowl over a larger bowl filled with ice so that the custard cools down, and the eggs do not cook.

Let it cool for 10 minutes, continuously stirring, and then pour into ramekins or cups, half way filling them.

Place a Danish biscuit into each ramekin, then pour on top of the biscuit the rest of the pudding to fill the ramekin or cup.

# Lancashire Biscuits

These tiny little balls of sheer delight stuck together with jam are a special one. This recipe is one that we frequently do in our family and whoever bakes them has to make extra to send to all of us! Our kids enjoy them so much because they can grab a handful and stuff their mouths with them. It makes my mom and uncle so happy seeing our kids eat them like that because they say it reminds them of how they used to run to their mom's kitchen in Alexandria and grab a handful themselves. My grandma used to make these for my mom and her friends in small boxes to gobble down during the famed Alexandria picnics.

## SERVING SIZE
4–6
Makes about 1 kg of biscuits

## BASIC RECIPE USED
1 recipe Jam (refer to pages 27-28)

| all-purpose flour | 30 g | 2 tbsp |
|---|---|---|
| corn flour | 30 g | 2 tbsp |
| baking powder | 3 g | ½ tsp |
| unsalted butter, cold | 50 g | ¼ cup |
| powdered sugar | 70 g | 7 tbsp |
| egg | 50 g | 1 large |
| vanilla powder | 5 g | 1 tsp |

Preheat the oven to 180°C (356°F).

Prepare a baking tray brushed with butter and dusted with flour or lined with parchment paper.

Sift flour with corn flour and baking powder and set aside.

In a hand-held electric mixer with the paddle attachment, beat the butter and sugar until fluffy.

Add egg and vanilla.

Add the dry ingredients and mix just until dough forms. If you feel the dough is too soft add more flour a tablespoon at a time, but don't add more than ¼ cup. If you still feel it is soft, wrap it in cling film and put it in the freezer for about 10 minutes or in the fridge for 30 minutes.

Form small pea-sized balls and place lightly on the cookie sheet, continue to do so placing all the tiny cookies side by side until you've used up all the dough.

Bake for 12–15 minutes. The cookies should be lightly browned at the bottom, but still pale on top.

Let them cool down on the baking sheet for 5 minutes before transferring to a rack to cool completely.

To assemble, stick 2 cookies together with your favourite jam.

## SERVING AND STORING SUGGESTIONS

They will last, unassembled, for up to 2 weeks in an airtight container at room temperature.

## TIPS AND TRICKS

*Once the cookies are filled, they will get soggy within 2–3 days.*

*If you want to keep them fresh, don't assemble them until ready to eat.*

# How to assemble a Lancashire biscuit

Place one cookie flat side up.

Add ½ tsp of jam to the center.

Place another cookie on top of the jam to sandwich it.

# Summer

Soaring temperatures. Hot winds. Wilting everything. Those are the images that a regular Middle Eastern summer might conjure up for you. Not in Alexandria. Alexandria has a cooler Mediterranean climate, unlike the rest of Egypt. Temperatures in summer are not as hot as Cairo or elsewhere. The beach, of course, is the best place to be by during summers. The water is perfect to just dip your feet in while sipping on cooling lemonade or to dive into, if you are an explorer looking to get a peek of ancient ruins. The reefs along the coast flaunt their best colours and shoals of beautiful fish playfully flit by. Swimming. Granitas. Beach-time. Yummy food. Summer, indeed, is a fun time to create memories.

Mother's memories of summer in Alexandria are of long days at the famous Montaza beach, gathered with all her friends with sand in her feet and hair and cheerful smiles on their faces, of uncontrollable giggles and of sand castles as only children can make. They would spend the entire day at the beach while her mother prepared food for the entire block by their beach cabana. She says it was a non-stop feast from breakfast to dinner as the sun set over the glorious waters.

Trays of food and desserts would be set along the length of their main table – a long, long table that my grandma set up right in front of the cabana. The table would always be laden and, Mother says, anyone passing by could – and would – stop for a bite. They would be cheerily welcomed and served before they strolled off on their way.

Summer, mother says with a faraway look in her eyes, reminds her of the sweet flavours of fresh cream and decadent biscuits. And of tea time, which was a must. Every day, by 5 p.m., my grandma would set up a fresh tray of sablés and cakes and hot tea for her friends and her to enjoy by the beach. Of course, my mom and her friends would run for the fresh treats!

My mom remembers summer treats so fondly, especially the freshness of the whipped cream and the crisp chocolate-filled sablés, which are her favourite, that these are staples on our beach table even today when she takes my boys out to the beach in summers.

May these summer treats create special memories for you too.

# Chocolate Sablé

The name sablé means sand in French, pointing to the sandy texture of these delicious cookies that crumble easily. Sablé cookies are basically France's version of a shortbread cookie, also called a butter cookie. Sablés can be made plain, dipped in chocolate or with jam. Chocolate sablés were my mom's favourite. She says her mother, my grandma, would shape parchment paper into cones and fill them with the sablé chocolate glaze. My mom would tear the tip of the parchment cone with her teeth to let the glaze fall into her mouth. Mother says she can still taste the chocolate!

## SERVING SIZE

Serves 10
Makes about 1 kg biscuits

## BASIC RECIPES USED

1 recipe Whipped Chocolate
Ganache (refer to page 2)
1 recipe Ganache Glaze
(refer to page 4)

| | | |
|---|---|---|
| unsalted butter, cold | 460 g | 2 cups |
| powdered sugar | 200 g | 1½ cups |
| egg yolks | 100 g | 6 large |
| all-purpose flour | 590 g | 4½ cups |
| unsweetened cocoa powder | 40 g | 4 tbsp |

Preheat the oven to 180°C (356°F).

Line a baking sheet with parchment paper or a silicone mat.

In a hand-held electric mixer with the paddle attachment, beat the butter and sugar together on medium speed for about 3 minutes until light and fluffy.

Add egg yolks and mix on medium speed until they are well incorporated. Stop to scrape the bowl with a rubber spatula before resuming the mixing.

Add the flour and cocoa powder and mix just until the dough is formed.

Wrap the dough in cling film and refrigerate for about 30 minutes. Lightly flour your counter top and roll the dough with your hands into a big ball.

Sprinkle some flour on top of the dough and use a rolling pin to roll the dough out. As soon as the dough starts sticking to your pin, sprinkle a pinch of flour on the dough, then resume rolling. Roll your dough out until it's approximately 0.5 cm (0.2 in) thick.

Use medium-sized round cookie cutters to cut out round cookies from the dough.

With a sharp-edged spatula transfer the cookie rounds onto the baking sheet. Make sure the cookies are spaced on the tray around 2 cm (1 in) from each other.

Bake for around 15 minutes.

Transfer the cookies to a wire rack and allow them to cool completely.

*Continued >*

The sablés will last in an
airtight container at room
temperature for 4–5 days.

The biscuits without filling
can last up to 2 weeks in an
airtight container.

## TO MAKE THE FILLING

Put the ganache in a piping bag using a small round piping tip and loosely tie the top of the bag.

Pipe each sablé biscuit with a dollop of ganache and then place another biscuit on top.

Alternately, you can spoon a teaspoon of ganache onto the centre of half the biscuits.

## TO GLAZE

Dip the top of the filled biscuits in the melted glaze.

Holding the biscuit upside down, lightly flick your hand or tap the biscuit to remove excess glaze.

## TIPS AND TRICKS

*When the dough is cold, it is easier to work with it.*

*If you are making sablés filled with jam with this recipe (like in the variations mentioned below), then leave half the sablé cookies complete and on the other half, use a smaller round cookie cutter to make a hole in the middle of the biscuit. If you don't have a smaller cookie cutter, use any small bottle cap.*

*The less you work the dough, the more tender and delicate the cookies will be.*

## VARIATIONS

You could make a **jam and sugar sablé**. To make this, replace the cocoa powder with 5 ml (1 tsp) vanilla extract, 5 g lemon zest (zest of 1 lemon) and add 3 g (½ tsp) salt.

- Choose the jam of your choice.
- Use a piping bag to pipe a dollop of jam on to the complete biscuit.
- Before adding the other half of the biscuit, sprinkle powdered sugar on it and place it gently on top of the biscuit that has jam.
- If the smaller whole is empty, add more jam.

You could also make sablés without any filling. Simply whisk an egg yolk with ¼ tsp vanilla and brush the tops of the basic biscuit.

# How to assemble a sablé

Use medium-sized round cookie cutters to cut out round cookies from the dough.

After baking and once completely cooled, pipe each sablé biscuit with a dollop of ganache and then place another biscuit on top.

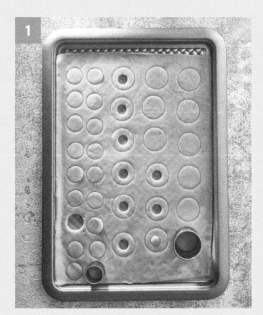

For a jam and sugar variation, use medium-sized round cookie cutters to cut out round cookies from the dough, then use a smaller round cookie cutter to make a hole in the middle.

After baking and once completely cooled, use a piping bag to pipe a dollop of jam on to the complete biscuit. Before adding the other half of the biscuit, sprinkle powdered sugar on it and place it gently on top of the biscuit that has jam.

# Simple Yogurt Cake

Who doesn't love moist cake?! The yogurt makes this cake extra moist and when the syrup soaks, it becomes extra juicy and sweet.

## SERVING SIZE

8–10 slices

## FOR THE SYRUP

| | | |
|---|---|---|
| white granulated sugar | 170 g | ⅔ cup |
| water | 115 ml | ½ cup |
| orange zest | 10 g | 2 tsp |

## FOR THE CAKE

| | | |
|---|---|---|
| all-purpose flour | 195 g | 1½ cup |
| baking powder | 5 g | 1 tsp |
| orange zest (optional) | 10 g | 1 tbsp |
| salt | 2 g | ¼ tsp |
| unsalted butter at room temperature | 170 g | ¾ cup |
| white granulated sugar | 260 g | 1 cup |
| eggs | 150 g | 3 large |
| vanilla extract | 5 g | 1 tsp |
| full-fat plain yogurt | 245 g | 1 cup |

### SERVING AND STORING SUGGESTIONS

The cake is best served while still warm, but it will last at room temperature, covered, for up to a week.

### TO MAKE THE CAKE SYRUP

In a small saucepan, combine sugar, water and orange zest.

Bring to a simmer over medium-high heat.

Cook for about 5 minutes or until the sugar has dissolved and syrup thickens. Set the syrup aside to cool.

### TO MAKE THE YOGURT CAKE

Preheat the oven to 180°C (356°F).

Prepare a 24 cm (9 in) round cake pan. Lay parchment paper on its base or brushed with butter and dusted with flour.

In a large bowl, whisk together flour, baking powder, orange zest and salt.

In another large bowl, using a hand-held electric mixer with the paddle attachment, beat the butter and sugar for about 3 minutes or until light in color.

Slowly add eggs and vanilla, one at a time, beating well after each addition.

Set the mixer on low speed and alternately beat in the flour mixture and yogurt, beginning and ending with the flour.

Pour the batter into the prepared pan.

Bake for 50–60 minutes or until the cake is golden and a toothpick inserted in the centre comes out clean.

Pour half the syrup over the cake and allow it to soak up the syrup.

Cool completely before turning it out on the serving platter.

Use the rest of the syrup to serve on the side.

### TIPS AND TRICKS

*To make sure the cake is extra moist and soaks up all the sugar syrup, poke holes using a fork or toothpick all around the cake as soon as it comes out of the oven and right before pouring the syrup.*

# Cheesecake

The much-loved cheesecake was born even before humans were weaving cloth, or could write cookbooks! Legend has it that during the 1st ever Olympic Games in 776 BC, cheesecakes were given to the sportsmen for the strength they needed to compete. This original energy food travelled around the world. Today, almost every country from Germany to Japan, from Italy to Chicago, has its own take on the cheesecake.

## SERVING SIZE

Serves 8–10 people

## FOR THE CRUST

1 recipe Graham Crackers
(refer page 7)

| | | |
|---|---|---|
| unsalted butter, melted | 50 g | ⅓ cup |

## FOR THE CHEESECAKE

| | | |
|---|---|---|
| eggs, separated | 150 g | 3 large |
| cream cheese, at room temperature | 650 g | 3 cups |
| white granulated sugar | 130 g | ½ cup |
| heavy cream | 55 g | ¼ cup |
| 1 vanilla bean | or 5 ml vanilla extract | or 1 tsp vanilla extract |
| Zest of 1 lemon (optional) | | |

Prepare a 24 cm (9 in) round springform pan with foil sealing the bottom and another larger baking sheet or pan in order to bake the cheesecake in a water bath (see Tips and Tricks).

### TO MAKE THE CRUST:

Break the graham crackers into small pieces by hand and place in a food processor and add the melted butter. Grind until the crackers have turned into sandy crumbs.

Test with your hands if the crust holds well together. If not, add a little more butter, a tablespoon at a time, until the crust mixture holds well together.

Then spread it out on the base of the pan pressing tightly with the palm of your hand to make sure all the crust is compressed together.

Completely cover the base and sides, leaving about 2–3 cm (1 in) of the sides all around.

### TO MAKE THE CHEESECAKE:

Preheat the oven to 180°C (356°F).

Using the bowl of a hand-held electric mixer with the whisk attachment, beat the egg whites on high speed until stiff peaks form (refer page xi)

Transfer the egg whites to a separate bowl.

Using the same bowl and whisk attachment (you don't need to clean the equipment), beat together the cream cheese and sugar until fluffy.

In a separate small bowl, whisk by hand, the egg yolks, cream, vanilla bean and lemon zest.

Add this to the cream cheese mixture and beat with the electric mixer for another minute.

*Continued >*

Chocolate variation: You can use the Chocolate Sablé biscuit recipe (refer to page 107) for the crust, and garnish the cheesecake with ganache.

If you want the cheesecake itself to be chocolate as well, add 20 gm (2 tbsp) of cocoa powder with the egg yolks and cream.

### SERVING AND STORING SUGGESTIONS

Cheesecake needs a little bit of planning ahead, it is best eaten the day *after* baking because it needs time to set and it is much easier to cut.

Just before serving, top the cheesecake evenly using a spatula with cheesecake toppings, chocolate ganache, or even jams. We love ours plain.

It will last up to 3 days in the fridge. Make sure your cheesecake is completely covered or in an airtight container.

Using a spatula or spoon, gently fold in the egg whites mixture until just incorporated. Pour into the crust.

Keep boiling water ready and pour it in the larger baking pan or tray. Refer to the tips section for how much water to add. Set the cheesecake gently inside the water and make sure it is comfortably set.

Bake in the water bath for around 40 minutes or until it has set. Halfway through, check on it and if the water seems to have decreased, just add a little more boiling water.

Once done, turn off the oven and open the door. Let it cool.

Once completely cooled, wrap the cheesecake very well in cling film and let it cool in the fridge overnight or in the freezer for a couple of hours before taking it out of the pan.

### TIPS AND TRICKS

*The problem with most cheesecakes is that they end up dry or too soft in the centre and well-cooked on the sides. The most important thing about the process of baking a cheesecake is that the temperature needs to stay constant. Any sudden changes in the oven temperature can affect the overall consistency of the cheesecake.*

*The best way to bake a cheesecake is in a water bath. Make sure you don't put too much water. It should be just enough for the cheesecake pan to settle nicely inside. You don't want too little water as that will just evaporate in the oven, but also not so much that the pan swims in it.*

*To completely protect your cheesecake from water entering it, use a springform baking pan and tightly cover the bottom of the springform pan with a layer or 2 of foil to make sure no water goes in. Make sure the foil is tight all around the base and goes up the sides around 5 cm (2 in).*

*Once it's done, turn off the oven, open the oven door slightly and keep the cheesecake inside the oven for 5-10 minutes before very carefully turning it out on a wire rack to completely cool. This way you will be sure it gradually and evenly bakes from the steam of the hot water. It also reduces the risk of having cracks on the surface.*

*I like my cheesecake to be completely white, so I don't like leaving it too long in the oven to avoid a golden color.*

*Don't take the cheesecake out of the springform pan unless it has been in the fridge for at least 6–8 hours. Otherwise, it could collapse or the pieces from the edges might stick to the sides of the pan.*

# Strawberry Birthday Cake

Strawberry shortcake parties became popular in the United States around 1850, as a celebration of the coming of summer. The 2012 Pasadena Strawberry Festival featured the world's largest strawberry shortcake. The cake used 3,240 pounds of strawberries and 280 pounds of whipped cream icing.

**SERVING SIZE**
Makes 10–12 slices

**BASIC RECIPES USED**
1 recipe Pastry Cream
(refer to page 15)
1 recipe Chiffon Cake, divided into
3 layers (refer to Chiffon Cake
recipe, page 24, for recipe and
page xiii for tips on how to slice
the cake)

| heavy cream | 600 g | 2½ cups |
|---|---|---|
| white granulated sugar | 130 g | ½ cup |
| orange juice* | 250 ml | 1 cup |
| fresh strawberries, diced | 500 g | 3 cups |

Using a hand-held electric mixer with the whisk attachment, whisk the heavy cream and sugar on high speed until firm peaks form (refer to page xi).

To assemble the cake, place 1 layer of the chiffon cake on the serving platter you will be using.

Using a silicon brush, moisten the layer evenly with the sugar water or orange juice.

Add 2 tablespoons of pastry cream and 1 tablespoon of the whipped cream to the centre of the base and lightly spread it.

Sprinkle ⅓rd of the diced strawberries in the centre.

Add the second cake layer and repeat the process.

Add the last cake layer and moisten with the liquid. Do not add the pastry cream at this stage.

Cover the entire cake and sides with the whipped cream.

Use the rest of the strawberries to decorate the top of the cake.

Sprinkle the top with powdered sugar using a sifter.

**TIPS AND TRICKS**

*Be careful to not spread too much of the pastry cream on the base cake, as when you add the second layer of the cake, it will make the layer of cream/filling spread.*

*You could also use whole or half strawberries to decorate the sides and top of the cake.*

*You can add toasted, sliced almonds to the sides of the cake.*

*For an alternative to orange juice use 250 ml (1 cup) water mixed with 20 g (2 tbsp) white granulated sugar.

**SERVING AND STORING SUGGESTIONS**

The cake will last, covered, in the refrigerator for up to 2 days.

# Super Simple Ice Cream Recipe

The meaning of the name 'ice cream' varies from one country to another. Terms such as 'frozen custard', 'frozen yogurt', 'sorbet', 'gelato' and others are used to distinguish different varieties and styles. In some countries, such as the United States, 'ice cream' applies only to a specific variety. In other countries, such as Italy and Argentina, one word is used for all variants.

**SERVING SIZE**

6–8 people

**FOR THE ICE CREAM**

| | | |
|---|---|---|
| heavy cream | 500 ml | 2¼ cups |
| vanilla extract | 5 ml | 1 vanilla bean or 1 tsp |
| sweetened condensed milk | 395 g | 1¼ cup (or 1 tin) |

**FOR THE CARAMELISED PISTACHIO**

| | | |
|---|---|---|
| raw & unsalted pistachios | 200 g | 1½ cups |
| white granulated sugar | 130 g | ½ cup |

Using a hand held electric mixer with the whisk attachment, whisk cream and vanilla bean to stiff peak stage (refer to page xi).

Fold in the condensed milk with a rubber spatula.

Place in the freezer for about an hour till partially set.

Remove from freezer and fold in any toppings you like (see variations).

Put back in the freezer and leave overnight or for at least 6–8 hours to freeze.

**TO CARAMELIZE THE PISTACHIOS**

Place the sugar in a saucepan on medium heat until it starts to turn gold.

With a wooden spoon or spatula, mix in the pistachios and make sure they are completely covered in sugar.

Pour it on a silicon sheet or parchment paper to completely cool.

Break it apart by hand or crush it with a rolling pin and fold it in the ice cream.

**TIPS AND TRICKS**

*To crush the pistachios, place a silicon sheet or parchment paper on your working surface, place the pistachios, then place another sheet on top to cover them. Now, crush the pistachios using a rolling pin.*

*Make sure you freeze the ice cream in the bowl you want to serve it in, because you won't be able to move it in another serving bowl after it is frozen.*

*Continued >*

## SERVING AND STORING SUGGESTIONS

The ice cream will last completely covered in the freezer for about 10 days, but once served, you cannot refreeze it.

Serve right away if you take out from the freezer – it does melt fast.

You can serve with warm chocolate ganache on the side.

## VARIATIONS

This is perfect served with souffle or brownies.

You can even make cookie ice cream sandwiches with it.

You can also mix in ganache glaze to make a chocolate ice cream.

- Add a tablespoon of chocolate at a time after folding in the condensed milk and try it.
- Keep adding the chocolate glaze until you reach the chocolate flavour you like.

Once it is partially set, you can add:

- A cup of fresh cut fruit.
- Toasted almond flakes (around 200 g/2 ½ cups).
- Caramelized pistachios (see recipe above).

If you're adding anything in the ice cream, make sure you fold the ingredient in well so it is mixed thoroughly in all of the ice cream.

# Granita

Granita is a semi-frozen dessert made from sugar, water and various flavourings, just as perfect for cool climes as it is for sweltering summers.

## SERVING SIZE

Serves 4–6

| juice of any fresh fruit you like | 500 ml | 2 cups |
|---|---|---|
| white granulated sugar | 195 g | ¾ cup |
| gelatin | 20 g | 2 tbsp |

### SERVING AND STORING SUGGESTIONS

A granita is best served right away.

Mix everything together in a bowl and leave overnight in the freezer to completely freeze.

In the morning, break with a spoon to make slush-like pieces or blend for a couple of seconds in a blender.

### VARIATIONS

We like using mangos, a mix of berries, or lemon with mint for juice.

You can also do a pink lemonade (a red berry and lemon) or strawberry with 1 tsp rose water.

# Banoffee Pie

Banoffee pie is an English dessert pie made from bananas, cream and toffee (made from boiled condensed milk, or dulce de leche), combined either on a buttery biscuit base or one made from crumbled biscuits and butter. Some versions of the recipe also include chocolate, coffee or both. Its name, sometimes spelled 'banoffi', is a portmanteau combining the words 'banana' and 'toffee'.

**SERVING SIZE**

8–10 servings

**BASIC RECIPE USED**

1 recipe Danish Biscuits
(refer to page 9)
50 g (⅓ cup) unsalted butter, melted

**FOR THE BANOFFEE**

| | | |
|---|---|---|
| sweetened condensed milk | 790 g | 2 ½ cups (or 2 tins) |
| heavy cream | 1 litre | 4 cups |
| white granulated sugar | 30 g | 3 tbsp |
| bananas | 1 kg | 7 |
| unsweetened cocoa powder | 50 g | ½ cup |

Prepare a 40 × 24 cm (16 × 10 in) Pyrex dish (oval or rectangular, depending on what you have).

Boil the cans of condensed milk on low heat, while still sealed, for 2–3 hours prior to beginning the rest of the preparation.

Once the condensed milk is ready and cooled, place the biscuits in a food processor to grind them together.

Add the melted butter and mix it with a spoon. Hold with your hands if the biscuits are falling apart. Add more melted butter, a tablespoon at a time, until they are firm together when holding.

Flatten the biscuits tightly on the Pyrex tray you prepared.

Pour the condensed milk on top of the crust and even it out so it is all 1 layer.

Whip the cream in a hand-held mixer with a whisk attachment with 2–3 tablespoons of sugar until stiff peaks form (refer to page xi). Be careful not to over-mix the cream as it can easily turn into butter.

Once all this is done, slice the bananas and layer them on top of the condensed milk.

Spoon over them the whipped cream as the final layer.

You can sprinkle shaved chocolate or cocoa powder on top for decoration.

**TIPS AND TRICKS**

*For the banoffee, we like to keep the Danish Biscuits in the oven a little longer until they are golden brown.*

# How to assemble a banoffee pie

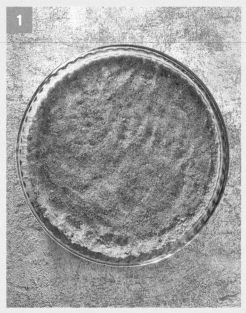

1

2

Flatten the biscuits tightly on the Pyrex tray you prepared.

Pour the condensed milk on top of the crust and even it out so it is all one layer.

3

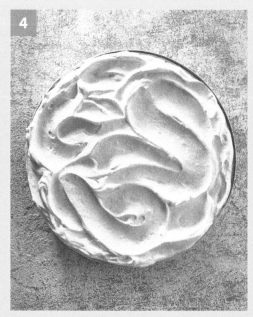

4

Slice the bananas and layer them on top of the condensed milk.

Spoon over the whipped cream as the final layer.

# Crème Caramel

Crème caramel, flan, or caramel custard is a custard dessert with a layer of clear caramel sauce, contrasted with crème brûlée, which is custard with a hard caramel layer on top. Crème caramel is a variant of plain custard (crème) where sugar syrup cooked to caramel stage is poured into the mould before adding the custard base.

## SERVING SIZE

4–6 servings

## FOR THE CRÈME BASE

| full cream milk | 560 ml | 2½ cups |
|---|---|---|
| 1 vanilla bean | or 5 ml vanilla extract | or 1 tsp vanilla extract |
| eggs | 100 g | 2 large |
| egg yolks | 80 g | 4 |
| white granulated sugar | 130 g | ½ cup |

## FOR THE CARAMEL:

| white granulated sugar | 195 g | ¾ cup |
|---|---|---|
| water | 60 ml | ¼ cup |

Using a silicon brush, brush 6 oven-proof ramekins with melted butter and set aside.

### TO MAKE THE CARAMEL

Using another saucepan, put the sugar for the caramel and add water just to barely cover the sugar on medium heat until it simmers.

Continue to cook until it thickens, starts toasting and turns to a deep golden colour.

Using a tablespoon, add the caramel to the base of each ramekin, make sure the entire base is covered.

### TO MAKE THE CRÈME BASE

Put the milk and vanilla into a small saucepan on medium heat.

Once it starts to simmer, remove from heat, cover it and set it aside.

In a separate bowl, add the eggs and yolks and whisk together using a hand whisk.

Add the sugar and whisk until it's incorporated.

Slowly add the warm milk to the egg and sugar mixture while continuously whisking.

Set it aside for about 10–15 minutes.

Meanwhile, preheat the oven to 180°C (356°F).

After leaving the custard to settle, it would have formed a foam at the top. Skim that foam from the surface using a spoon and discard.

*Continued >*

It will last, covered, in the fridge for up to 3 days.

Before serving, put the bottom of the ramekin on direct heat or in a baking tray with boiling water for a couple of minutes to melt the caramel before unmoulding it.

To unmould, run a knife around the insides of each ramekin then flip onto a serving platter.

Using a sieve to make sure there are no lumps, pour the custard into the ramekins.

Cover each one with foil and place in a deep baking pan.

Pour hot water in the pan, up to ⅔rds of the ramekins.

Bake in the oven for 15 minutes, then remove the foil and bake for another 10 minutes or until the custard is set but remains slightly wobbly at the centre.

Let it cool completely and then refrigerate for a couple of hours or overnight.

### TIPS AND TRICKS

*To check if the caramel is done, take it off the heat and put a tiny bit on a plate. If it hardens right away then it is done.*

*Work quickly with the caramel as it can set and harden very fast.*

# Black Forest Cake

Black Forest cake is a chocolate sponge cake with a rich cherry filling based on the German dessert Schwarzwälder Kirschtorte. Typically, Black Forest cake consists of several layers of chocolate sponge cake sandwiched with whipped cream and cherries. It is decorated with additional whipped cream, maraschino cherries and chocolate shavings. In some European traditions, sour cherries are used both between the layers and for decorating the top.

## SERVING SIZE

Serves 10–12

## BASIC RECIPE USED

1 recipe chocolate Sponge Cake, divided into 3 layers (refer to Sponge Cake chocolate variation on page 23 and tips on how to divide cakes on page xiii)

| heavy cream | 600 ml | 2 ½ cups |
|---|---|---|
| white granulated sugar | 30 g | ¼ cup |
| water mixed with white granulated sugar | 260 ml/ 20 g | 1 cup / 2 tbsp |

## OTHER REQUIREMENTS

2 cans sweet cherries in syrup, halved
Preserved syrup of cherry cans
1 recipe Chocolate Ganache Glaze (optional, refer to page 4 for recipe) OR 50 g (½ cup) cocoa powder

## SERVING AND STORING SUGGESTIONS

The cake will last, covered, in the refrigerator for up to 3 days.

Using a hand-held electric mixer with the whisk attachment, whisk the heavy cream and sugar on high speed until stiff peaks form (refer to page xi).

To assemble the cake, place 1 cake layer on the serving platter you will be using.

Using a silicon brush, lightly moisten the layer evenly with the sugar water. Then brush with a little cherry syrup.

Add 3 tablespoons of the whipped cream to the centre of the base and lightly spread it.

Sprinkle ⅓rd of the halved cherries on top of the cream, and drizzle with a tablespoon of syrup again.

Add the second cake layer on top and repeat the process.

Add the last cake layer, moistening it with sugar water and cherry syrup.

Spread the remaining whipped cream on top and all around the sides to cover the entire cake, making sure to smoothen out the cream throughout the sides.

Decorate the cake by pouring chocolate ganache glaze on top or you can sprinkle cocoa powder using a sifter on top the cream.

Finally, decorate the top with the remaining cherries.

### TIPS AND TRICKS

*Be careful not to add too much of the whipped cream to the centre of the cake base, as when you add the second layer it will spread out.*

*Make sure you refrigerate for at least 30 minutes before serving to allow it time to set.*

# Summer Trifle

The much loved, much experimented with, much overused trifle has changed over centuries in appearance, ingredients and taste, just as it has changed in its spelling!

What started as the pride of European lunch and high-tea tables started being made with synthetic ingredients and thus got relegated to the lower tier of dessert trays.

When made well, however, the trifle is still a tasty treat!

**SERVING SIZE**

10–12 people

**BASIC RECIPE USED**

1 recipe Basic Ladyfingers
(refer to page 20)

| | | |
|---|---|---|
| heavy cream | 500 ml | 2 ½ cups |
| granulated white sugar | 50 g | ¼ cup |
| fresh orange juice | 500 ml | 2 ½ cups |
| sliced fruit of choice | 500 g | 4 cups |

Prepare a deep-dish glass serving bowl.

In the bowl of a hand-held electric mixer with the whisk attachment, beat the cream and sugar well until the cream is whipped at stiff peaks (refer to page xi).

Dip the biscuits in orange juice, making sure all sides are properly dipped for about 2-3 seconds.

Layer the bowl with biscuits, cream and slices of fruit. We like to use mangos or strawberries, depending on the season.

Top with cream and a drizzle of fruits in the centre.

**TIPS AND TRICKS**

*You can add a vanilla bean to the cream while whisking. The little black vanilla dots always make a prettier trifle (but not necessary if you don't have them).*

*Taste the cream. If you would like it sweeter, add more sugar.*

*Once the cream reaches stiff peaks, stop beating right away. If the cream gets over-mixed it will turn into butter!*

*Make sure you do not dip the biscuits in the juice for more than 2-3 seconds, or else they will get mushy.*

**VARIATIONS**

You can use sweetened lemon juice or mango juice instead of orange.

**SERVING AND STORING SUGGESTIONS**

Once the trifle is layered, it is best served right away. It usually won't last longer than a day.

# Éclairs

The éclair originated during the nineteenth century in France where it was called 'pain à la Duchesse' or 'petite duchesse' until 1850. Some food historians speculate that éclairs were first made by Antonin Carême (1784–1833), the famous French chef.

## SERVING SIZE

Serves 10–12
Yields about 15 éclairs

## BASIC RECIPES USED

1 recipe Choux Pastry (refer to page 13 for ingredients; see piping instructions in the method)
1 recipe Pastry Cream (refer to page 15; divide into ½ chocolate ½ vanilla)
1 recipe Chocolate Ganache Glaze (refer to page 4)

Preheat oven to 180°C (356°F).

Prepare baking tray lined with parchment paper or greased with butter and dusted with flour.

Prepare Choux Pastry dough and follow below instructions for éclairs shapes.

Use a wide (French) star tip to pipe 10 cm (4 in) long logs side by side on the prepared baking tray, leaving about 2 cm (1 in) between 2 logs.

Keep the ends of the logs just a little thicker than the centre.

Bake for around 30 minutes until golden.

Allow them to cool, then poke the bottom of each choux using the tip of the piping hole to make 3 holes – 1 on each end and 1 in the middle.

Fill half the éclair with chocolate pastry cream and the other half with vanilla.

Dip the tops with chocolate ganache glaze, making sure you cover the entire top surface.

### TIPS AND TRICKS

*If the choux becomes too crisp while baking, place in an airtight container in the freezer for a couple of hours or overnight and then defrost for them to soften up.*

### SERVING AND STORING SUGGESTIONS

Allow the éclairs to set in the refrigerator for about an hour before serving.

They can be stored in an airtight container in the refrigerator for up to 3 days.

# Autumn

The weather in autumn in Alexandria is pleasant and peaceful.

What makes autumn so special was that the holy month of Ramadan came in autumn back when my mother was growing up. Given my grandma's love – and talent – for cooking, it should come as no surprise that every day of Ramadan was a feast. And, of course, there was dessert!

Ramadan is a time to introspect as much as it is a time to gather with family. The tradition of eating together at Suhoor, the meal before beginning the fast and at Iftar, the meal after breaking the fast, is a beautiful one as it is really the time for everyone to get together and bond. In our family, no one would even think of another place to be at, other than my grandma's, for Iftar. Every day at sunset, for the 30 days of Ramadan, all my mother's uncles, aunts and cousins would gather to break their fast over my grandma's huge, elegant and well-laden dining table. They would break their fast over dates soaked in milk. Right after, the whole family would stand in prayer together. They would then sit for the feast grandma had created and they would stay at the dining table for hours, eating and talking until the next prayer time. My mother still remembers the sounds of all the kids running around during Iftar, adding to the feeling of festivity and the whole family gathering over her mom's delicious feasts. They would go out to the living room afterwards to enjoy the Ramadan specials on TV, while sipping on their tea/coffee (and milk for the kids!) and a second, sometimes third, round of dessert. Till date, whenever we gather for Iftar, everyone, from those of my grandma's time to my cousins, talks fondly of my grandma's Iftar feasts.

This section is dedicated to Middle Eastern treats as this is specifically when my grandma would bake Oriental desserts every day.

My mom's description of autumn as growing up is of the sweetness of syrup soaking in desserts and dripping on her plate and the crunchiness that comes with every bite of Baklava!

Happy, warm memories. Much like autumn.

# Cream-filled Kunafa

Kunafa is a traditional Middle Eastern dessert made with shredded filo pastry, a soaked in a sweet, sugar-based syrup and typically layered with cheese, or with other ingredients such as clotted cream or nuts, depending on the region. Kunafa is really best served hot with fresh pistachios on top.

With its flaky crust, warm melted sweet cream in the middle and fragrant syrup poured on top, we've all been guilty of having seconds (or thirds)! It is a family favorite all year round, and especially during the holy month of Ramadan.

## SERVING SIZE
Makes 8–10

## BASIC RECIPE USED
1 recipe Simple Sugar Syrup
(refer to page 16)

## FOR THE KUNAFA BASE

| | | |
|---|---|---|
| kunafa dough | 500 g | 7 cups |
| ghee, melted | 200 g | 1 cup |

## FOR THE CREAM FILLING

| | | |
|---|---|---|
| corn flour | 60 g | ½ cup |
| water at room temperature | 60 ml | ¼ cup |
| full cream milk | 720 ml | 3 cups |
| white granulated sugar | 130 g | ½ cup |
| canned cream (puk, if you are in Egypt or in the Middle East) | 170 g | 1 cup |
| orange blossom water | 5 ml | 1 tsp |

Prepare a 24 cm (9 in) round baking tray greased with ghee.

### PREPARE THE CREAM FILLING

Have a bowl set aside next to you while working.

In a separate small bowl, add the corn flour to the water and mix until dissolved. Set aside.

In a medium-sized, deep saucepan, mix the milk and sugar over high heat. Continue mixing until the mixture comes to a boil.

Bring heat down to low and add the corn flour mixture. It should thicken immediately.

Continue mixing for another minute, then remove from heat.

Add in the cream and orange blossom while continuously whisking.

Once everything is incorporated, transfer to the bowl you had set aside and cover the surface with cling film and set it aside to cool.

### TO MAKE THE KUNAFA

Preheat oven at 180°C (356°F).

Very finely shred the kunafa dough by hand until the strands are maximum 2 cm (1 in) long.

Pour the melted ghee over the dough and, using your hands, mix and rub until all the kunafa dough is completely covered in ghee.

*Continued >*

Place about ⅔rds of the shredded dough on the base of the prepared baking tray covering the entire base. Use the palms of your hands to press firmly to make sure the dough is tightly compressed in the tray. Cover about 1 cm (0.5 in) up the sides as well.

Using a tablespoon, spoon out the cream onto the compressed kunafa dough and cover the entire base with cream.

Very gently, cover the top with the remaining kunafa dough. Press very lightly on the dough just to make sure the kunafa top is intact.

Place in the oven and bake for about 30–40 minutes until it is deep golden brown on the sides.

As soon as you bring it out, pour syrup all over, making sure to cover the entire surface.

Let it cool for 10–15 minutes and allow syrup to soak, then place it out on the serving platter.

### TIPS AND TRICKS

*When covering the cream, make sure the cling film is touching the surface, so it doesn't create a layer of skin at the top.*

*While working to shred the kunafa dough, make sure you cover any batches that were already shredded, or are waiting to be shredded, with a damp cloth as they can dry out very fast.*

*For a faster process, divide the kunafa into 3 batches and pulse each batch in the food processor for 5 seconds each.*

*When placing the dough in bottom of the pan, you can use a smaller, round baking tray, if available, to press the bottom of the tray on the dough to tightly compress it.*

*When filling the kunafa with the cream, make sure you use a tablespoon and spoon out the cream. Don't try to spread it around as it can move the dough, mixing the dough and cream together into one lump.*

*Be very careful when covering the top of the kunafa as the cream can bulge out.*

# How to assemble a kunafa

Place about ⅔rds of the shredded dough on the base of the prepared baking tray covering the entire base.

Using a tablespoon, spoon out the cream onto the compressed kunafa dough and cover the entire base with cream.

Very gently, cover the top with the remaining kunafa dough. Press very lightly on the dough just to make sure the kunafa top is intact.

# Date Tart

A Middle Eastern twist on fruit tarts. The crust is crisp and golden and the dates make it extra sweet with a little bit of caramelization when they bake in the oven.

**SERVING SIZE**

Serves 6–8

## FOR THE CRUST

| | | |
|---|---|---|
| unsalted butter | 325 g | 1½ cups |
| white granulated sugar | 250 g | 1¼ cups |
| egg | 50 g | 1 large |
| egg yolk | 20 g | 1 |
| lemon zest | 5 g | 1 tsp |
| vanilla extract | 5 ml | 1 tsp |
| all-purpose flour | 500 g | 3¾ cups |

## FOR THE ALMOND CRÈME

| | | |
|---|---|---|
| unsalted butter | 125 g | ½ cup + 1 tbsp |
| powdered sugar | 125 g | 1 cup |
| eggs | 150 g | 3 large |
| vanilla extract | 8 g | 1½ tsp |
| almond flour | 125 g | 1 cup |
| all-purpose flour | 50 g | ⅓ cup |

## FOR THE TOPPING

| | | |
|---|---|---|
| fresh rabbi dates, pitted, halved and skin removed | 500 g | 3 cups |
| apricot jam | 20 g | 2 tbsp |

Prepare a 20 cm (8 in) round fluted pie tray, greased with butter and dusted with flour.

In a hand-held electric mixer with the paddle attachment, beat butter and sugar on medium-high speed for 5 minutes until it becomes light and fluffy.

Lower speed to medium-slow and add egg and yolk, lemon zest, vanilla and salt and beat for another 2 minutes.

Lower to slow speed and gradually add the flour until all is incorporated.

Make the dough into a ball, wrap in cling film and place in the freezer for 10 minutes.

### IN THE MEANTIME, PREPARE THE ALMOND CREAM

In a hand-held electric mixer with the whisk attachment, beat the butter and sugar on high speed until they are well mixed together.

Lower speed to medium and add the eggs and vanilla.

Gradually add the almond flour and all-purpose flour. The mixture should be light and fluffy.

### TO ASSEMBLE

Once the almond crème is ready, preheat the oven to 180°C (356°F).

Take out the pie crust from the freezer and place it on a lightly floured surface.

Roll out dough using a rolling pin to about a 30 cm (12 in) round shape.

With the palm of your hands, start picking up the rolled-out dough from the bottom and very carefully transfer into the prepared pie tray. Gently press the dough into the edges.

Cut out any excess dough around the edges of the pie tray using scissors or a knife. Cover any cracks in the base with excess dough.

*Continued >*

**SERVING AND STORING
SUGGESTIONS**

It will last, covered, at
room temperature for up to
3 days.

Pour the prepared almond cream over the dough, filling up the entire base.

Start placing the halved dates one by one on top of the cream. They should be aligned next to each other, until you cover the entire pie.

Bake for about 20–30 minutes, until the edges start to crisp and become golden.

Allow the tart to cool for 10–15 minutes and if you used a tray with a removable bottom, then remove the bottom and set the pie on a serving platter.

Once completely cooled, brush the top of the dates with apricot jam.

### TIPS AND TRICKS

*If you didn't use removable bottom then leave it in the same tray, don't transfer.*

# Baked Rice Pudding

Rice puddings are found in nearly every area of the world. Recipes can greatly vary even within a single country. The dessert can be boiled or baked. Different types of pudding vary depending on preparation methods and the selected ingredients.

Especially on a dark, dreary day, its fragrant and creamy. This pudding is subtly sweet and easily adapts to your mood – whether you feel like a sprinkling of spicy cinnamon or you desire some plump, chewy raisins. It truly is one of the easiest puddings you can ever make, starting with a short ingredient list of kitchen staples and an infinite number of ways with which you can customize it.

**SERVING SIZE**

Serves 6–8

| | | |
|---|---|---|
| full cream milk | 1.7 l | 8½ cups |
| short grain white rice | 100 g | ½ cup |
| white granulated sugar | 260 g | 1 cup |
| vanilla extract | 10 ml | 1 tsp |
| mastic | 2 g | 3 pieces |
| corn starch | 10 g | 2 tsp |
| heavy cream | 240 ml | 1 cup |

Prepare a 22 cm (9 in) baking dish that is at least 5 cm (2 in) deep.

Reserve ¼ cup of milk on the side.

Rinse rice in cold water until the water comes out clear. Let the rice sit in a sieve for 5–10 minutes to drain out all the water.

In a large, deep saucepan, bring the milk to a boil.

Add the rice and lower heat. Stir with a wooden spoon after every couple of minutes.

Once the rice starts to absorb the milk, add in the sugar, vanilla and mastic.

Continue stirring for about 40 minutes until the milk is fully absorbed, the rice is cooked through and is of creamy consistency.

In a small bowl, combine the corn starch with the reserved milk and mix. Pour the corn starch mixture over the rice pudding on low heat.

Continue stirring until the mixture starts to thicken.

Add the heavy cream, mixing for another minute, before removing the saucepan from heat.

Transfer the rice pudding to the prepared baking dish and allow it to settle for about 10 minutes uncovered.

Meanwhile, preheat the oven broiler to 180°C (356°F).

Place the rice pudding in the top rack of the oven right under the broiler, until the top starts to bake into brownish/golden spots. This should take about 5–10 minutes.

*Continued >*

## SERVING AND STORING SUGGESTIONS

It is best enjoyed straight out of the oven, but it will last, covered, in the fridge for up to 3 days.

Remove from oven and let it cool on a wire rack for about 10 minutes before you enjoy.

### TIPS AND TRICKS

*You can use a ceramic or Pyrex dish if available as you will be serving the platter in the same dish.*

*Keep an eye on the pudding while broiling it as it can burn very fast.*

*While baking the pudding, turn the dish halfway through to get an evenly coloured top.*

# Milk Pudding

Did you know: In the United Kingdom the word 'pudding' is used to refer to any dessert. Desserts were the indulgences of the upper classes and included international cuisine like chocolate mousse, soufflé and Champagne jelly.

**SERVING SIZE**

Serves 8–10

**FOR THE PUDDING**

| whole milk | 1 litre | 5 cups |
|---|---|---|
| heavy cream | 360 ml | 1½ cups |
| white granulated sugar | 260 g | 1 cup |
| corn starch | 65 g | ½ cup |
| vanilla extract | 5 ml | 1 tsp |

**FOR THE TOPPING**

| unsalted toasted hazelnuts | 100 g | 1 cup |
|---|---|---|
| unsweetened shredded coconut | 50 g | ½ cup |
| golden raisins | 80 g | ½ cup |

Prepare 10 small ramekins.

In a large, deep saucepan, whisk the milk, heavy cream, sugar and corn starch on low heat until the corn starch and sugar completely dissolve.

Continue to whisk, raise the heat to high and bring the milk mixture to a boil.

Once it starts boiling, add in the vanilla.

Continue to let the milk boil for a few more seconds until the mixture thickens.

Once it thickens, remove from heat right away and continue whisking for a couple of minutes.

Pour into the ramekins and let it cool down for about 15 minutes.

Once cooled, refrigerate for 30 minutes, uncovered, until the surface has begun to set.

Cover it and let it refrigerate for a couple of hours or overnight before serving.

**TO MAKE THE TOPPING**

Lay the toasted hazelnuts on parchment paper and crush them using a rolling pin.

Mix all the topping ingredients together and serve in a separate bowl.

**TIPS AND TRICKS**

*Make sure you stir the milk mixture while it is on the heat in order not to get any lumps.*

*As soon as it thickens, immediately remove from heat so that it stays smooth. It will thicken more as it sets.*

**VARIATIONS**

Instead of the vanilla, you can add 1 tsp (5 ml) of rose water.

Use crushed raw pistachios as topping.

# Um Ali

Egypt's equivalent to bread pudding, this dessert is best served warm with cinnamon, dried fruits or nuts sprinkled on top. The warmth of the bread, the sweet dessert aroma and the addictive texture of the pudding are only a few of the reasons why this dessert will always remain a popular way to end a long day.

## SERVING SIZE
Serves 6–8

## BASIC RECIPE USED
1 recipe baked Flaky Pie Crust (refer to page 19)

## FOR THE MILK BASE

| full cream milk | 800 ml | 4 cups |
| --- | --- | --- |
| heavy cream | 200 ml | 1 cup |
| white granulated sugar | 200 g | 1 cup |
| fresh clotted cream | 360 ml | 1½ cups |

## FOR THE TOPPING

| toasted unsalted hazelnuts, coarsely chopped | 70 g | ½ cup |
| --- | --- | --- |
| raisins | 75 g | ½ cup |
| unsweetened shredded coconut | 20 g | 2 tbsp |

### SERVING AND STORING SUGGESTIONS

This dish is best served right away while hot.

Serve the topping in a separate bowl on the side.

Preheat the oven to 180°C (356°F).

Prepare a 22 cm (9 in) baking dish that is at least 5 cm (2 in) deep. You can use a ceramic or Pyrex dish, if available, as you will be serving the platter in the same dish.

Break half of the pie crust by hand into around 2 cm (1 in) pieces.

Place on top of each other, covering the entire base of the baking dish and set aside.

In a medium saucepan, stir the milk, heavy cream and sugar on high heat until the milk starts to boil. Stir continuously.

Once the milk boils, remove from heat right away and pour over the pie crust.

Use the remaining half of the crust to break and scatter on top of the milk.

Top the mixture with the clotted cream, 1 tablespoon at a time till the entire top is covered.

Turn the heated oven broiler on and leave it in for about 10 minutes, until it turns a deep golden brown.

Crisp for about 10 more minutes. You may need to rotate the dish halfway through to get an even-coloured top, so keep a close eye.

### TO MAKE THE TOPPING

Mix all the ingredients together in a bowl, and serve on the side.

### TIPS AND TRICKS

*When baking the pie crust, make sure to roll it very thin.*

*Let it bake till very golden and crisp for a little extra crunchiness.*

# Semolina Orange Cake

This is my grandma's simple invention. It's a cross between the basbousa and yogurt cake. This is a dry cake, moistened with a citrus syrup that makes it sweet and light.

**SERVING SIZE**
Serves 6–8

**BASIC RECIPE USED**
1 recipe Simple Syrup (refer to page 16). Add 10 g/1 tbsp orange zest) when making the syrup

| | | |
|---|---|---|
| all-purpose flour | 190 g | 1½ cups |
| coarse semolina | 220 g | 1¼ cups |
| baking powder | 5 g | 1 tsp |
| unsalted butter | 130 g | ½ cup |
| white granulated sugar | 390 g | 1½ cups |
| eggs | 150 g | 3 large |
| vanilla sugar | 5 g | 1 tsp |
| orange zest | 10 g | 1 tbsp |
| full cream milk | 390 ml | 1¾ cups |

Prepare the syrup and set aside to cool.

Preheat the oven to 180°C (356°F).

Prepare a 24 cm (9 in) round cake pan greased with butter and dusted with flour.

In a bowl, mix together the flour, semolina and baking powder and set aside.

In the bowl of a hand-held electric mixer with the paddle attachment, beat the butter and sugar on medium speed for about 3 minutes until light and fluffy.

Bring down to slow speed and add the eggs, one at a time, followed by the vanilla sugar and orange zest.

Start adding half the flour mixture, followed by half the milk and continue mixing until just incorporated. Repeat once more until everything is well mixed.

Pour the batter into the prepared pan and bake until the sides are golden and a knife comes out clean from the centre.

As soon as it is out of the oven, use a toothpick or fork to poke holes all around the cake.

Pour the cooled syrup right away, covering the entire cake.

Allow it to cool for about 15–20 minutes before turning it out onto a serving platter.

Pour more syrup to cover the top.

**TIPS AND TRICKS**

*The cake is best enjoyed a couple of hours after baking or on the next day so the syrup has time to soak in.*

**SERVING AND STORING SUGGESTIONS**

The cake will last up to 3 days in an airtight container at room temperature.

# Balah Al Sham

These churro-like, Middle Eastern fritters are crunchy on the outside and irresistibly squishy soft on the inside. As soon as they come out of the fryer, they get dipped in a pool of vanilla sugar syrup, which makes them delightfully squirty to the bite.

**SERVING SIZE**

10–12
Yields about 40 pieces

**BASIC RECIPE USED**

1 recipe Simple Sugar Syrup
(refer page 16)

| ghee | 30 g | 3 tbsp |
| --- | --- | --- |
| water | 180 ml | ¾ cup |
| all-purpose flour | 100 g | ¾ cup |
| salt | 2 g | ½ tsp |
| eggs | 100 g | 2 large |
| vanilla sugar | 10 g | 2 tsp |
| vegetable oil for frying | 500 ml | 2½ cups |

**TO MAKE THE DOUGH**

Prepare the syrup and set aside to cool.

In saucepan, using a hand whisk, beat together the ghee and water on high heat.

Once the liquid starts to boil, lower the heat and add the flour and salt.

Using a spatula, fold the mixture together. Continue folding until it starts to look/feel like a paste or pudding.

Remove from heat and put the mixture in a hand-held electric mixer, using the paddle attachment. Mix on medium speed. Keep mixing till it cools a bit.

Add in the eggs, vanilla and ghee, and mix until everything is well incorporated.

Fill a pastry bag, tipped with a wide (French) star tip, with the dough.

Meanwhile, pour oil into a large frying pan and heat on medium until it is just warm.

As soon as the oil starts to warm, start piping the dough directly into the oil.

Pipe the fingers about 5 cm (2 in) long and use scissors to cut through the dough while piping.

Make a few at a time so that you don't overcrowd the pan. You need to make space for them to expand while frying.

Flip them every couple of minutes, repeating the process until the dough is finished.

Fry until deep golden brown in colour.

Have a baking tray ready with paper towels and transfer the pastry to it to first drain out excess oil.

Then transfer to another baking tray without the paper towels.

While still hot, pour the cooled syrup on top of the pastry, flipping it to make sure all sides are covered in syrup.

*Continued >*

The *balah al sham* is best served warm or on the same day to enjoy their crunchiness.

If serving within a couple of hours, cover the top with aluminium foil and poke holes in it to maintain crunchiness.

Transfer to a sieve that has been placed over a bowl and allow any excess syrup to drip.

Assort them in a serving platter in any way you like. I like to layer them on top of each other.

## TIPS AND TRICKS

*When mixing the dough, make sure the dough cools down a bit before adding the eggs so the eggs don't cook.*

*If available, it is better to use a large star tip when piping, to get fat pieces that are crunchy on the outside and chewy on the inside.*

*To make sure you get the right consistency and crunchiness, don't overheat the oil, it should always be just warm to touch.*

*If the oil starts to boil, remove the pan from the heat and allow the oil temperature to drop down to warm, before piping again.*

# How to pipe balah al sham dough

As soon as the oil starts to warm, start piping the dough directly into the oil.

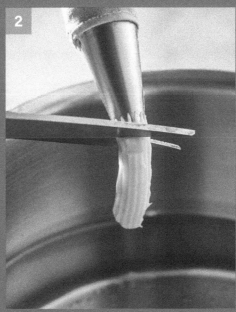

Pipe the fingers about 5 cm (2 in) long and use scissors to cut through the dough while piping.

# Hazelnut Baklava Fingers

Baklava is a delicious phyllo pastry popular in Middle Eastern countries. Its supposed origins are Turkish, dating to the Byzantine Empire (or even further), though many cultures claim it for their own.

## SERVING SIZE
10–12
Makes up to 100 fingers

## BASIC RECIPE USED
1 recipe Simple Sugar Syrup
(refer page 16)

## FOR THE PASTRY

| | | |
|---|---|---|
| unsalted toasted hazelnuts | 260 g | 2 cups |
| ghee or unsalted butter | 120 g | ½ cup |

1 pack phyllo pastry, thawed overnight in fridge

### SERVING AND STORING SUGGESTIONS

It is best enjoyed the same day.

The fingers will last in an airtight container for up to 2 days.

Prepare a baking tray greased with ghee.

Toast the hazelnuts in the oven on 180°C (356 F) for 10–15 minutes.

Place in a processor to finely grind them.

### TO MAKE THE BAKLAVA FINGERS

In the meantime, start working on the baklava fingers.

Preheat oven to 180°C (356 F).

Melt the ghee and keep it next to you as you are working.

Lay 1 phyllo sheet flat on your work surface and, using a silicon brush, brush all over with melted ghee.

Lay a second sheet on top and repeat.

Sprinkle 3 tablespoons of the hazelnuts evenly all over the sheet, keeping about 2 cm (1 in) from the edges.

Beginning from the edge closer to you, start rolling the phyllo tightly, pressing with your fingers, into skinny cigarette-like logs (see next page for images).

Cut the logs into 5 cm (2 in) fingers and lay on prepared baking tray.

Lay them alongside each other, do not leave space.

Repeat the process until you finish the filling.

Brush the tops with the melted butter or ghee and bake for 20–30 minutes until golden.

As soon as the tray comes out of the oven, cover the fingers entirely with the syrup.

### TIPS AND TRICKS

*Make sure you lay them seam-down so they remain tightly wrapped.*

*You may need to rotate the pans halfway through to make sure you get evenly baked fingers.*

*Continued >*

# How to roll baklava fingers

Sprinkle 3 tablespoons of the hazelnuts
evenly all over the sheet, keeping about
2 cm (1 in) from the edges.

Beginning from the edge closer to you, start
rolling the phyllo tightly, pressing with your
fingers, into skinny cigarette-like logs.

# Walnut Baklava

If you've ever eaten baklava, chances are you'd have fallen in love with this simple, yet richly delicious dessert. Drenched in honey syrup, yet crunchy because of the phyllo pastry and nuts, the Baklava (or baklawa or baclava) has enthralled the taste buds of people right from the Assyrian Empire as early as 8th century B.C. to across the globe today.

The original version of baklava was unleavened bread topped with nuts and doused with honey. The Ottoman Empire cooks refined it to a more sophisticated version during the 15th century. A cookbook recovered from a palace in the ancient city of Constantinople listed baklava as a favourite dessert, fit for royalty.

## SERVING SIZE
6–8

## FOR THE SYRUP

| | | |
|---|---|---|
| white granulated sugar | 260 g | 1 cup |
| honey | 320 ml | 1 cup |
| water | 220 ml | 1 cup |
| Juice and zest of 1 orange | | |
| 2 cinnamon sticks | | |

## FOR THE BAKLAVA FILLING

| | | |
|---|---|---|
| raw unsalted walnuts | 300 g | 2½ cups |
| white granulated sugar | 130 g | ½ cup |
| cinnamon powder | 15 g | 3 tsp |
| ghee or unsalted butter, melted | 800 g | 4 cups |
| 2 packs of frozen phyllo pastry, thawed in the fridge over night | | |

### TO MAKE THE SYRUP

Prepare the syrup and set aside to cool.

Place all ingredients together in a pot on high heat until its thickness becomes just a little lesser than the thickness of honey.

### TO MAKE THE BAKLAVA

Preheat the oven to 180°C (356°F).

Prepare a 24 cm (9 in) round baking tray, greasing it with ghee.

Crush the walnuts in a blender or food processor and put sugar on it, then add cinnamon.

Mix everything well with a spoon or spatula and set aside.

In the baking tray, layer 6 sheets of phyllo pastry on top of each other brushing each sheet with ghee before placing another on top. Apply ghee on the top sheet.

Spread a cup of the walnut mixture on top of these 6 sheets.

Add another 6 sheets of phyllo, applying ghee between each sheet and then spread a cup of walnuts like previously done.

Repeat until you have a total of 3 layers of the walnut filling then top with the last 6 layers of phyllo brushing each layer with ghee.

Cut into equal squares and bake in the oven for about 30 minutes, until it turns golden.

Pour the cooled syrup on top of the baklava as soon as it comes out of the oven. Wait until it's completely cooled to turn it out into your serving platter.

*Continued >*

## SERVING AND STORING SUGGESTIONS

Baklava is best eaten fresh out of the oven, but it will last for up to 2 days in an airtight container at room temperature.

## TIPS AND TRICKS

*For the syrup, I like to put the juice in and then add the entire orange as well, and when the syrup is ready, I just remove the orange peels.*

*The baklava should be hot and the syrup should be cold when it is poured on it so the baklava remains crunchy.*

*The beauty of baklava lies in the layering and brushing, so make sure you get the layers right.*

# How to assemble a baklava

1
Layer 6 sheets of phyllo pastry on top of each other brushing each sheet with butter before placing another on top. Apply butter on the top sheet.

2
Spread a cup of the walnut mixture on top of these 6 sheets.

3
Add another 6 sheets of phyllo, applying butter between each sheet and then spread a cup of walnuts like previously done. Repeat this process till you have a total of 3 layers of walnuts then cover with 6 phyllo pastry sheets and brush the topmost sheet with butter.

4
Cut into equal squares and bake in the oven for about 30 minutes, until it turns golden.

# Basbousa

Basbousa, an Egyptian semolina cake, is one of the best Egyptian desserts that comes out fairly quickly. This is an authentic Egyptian basbousa recipe. A delicious coconut and semolina/farina cake that gets sprinkled with nuts and drizzled with syrup to put on the final seal of perfection.

Basbousa/basboosa is a term in the Middle East that refers to a very sweet semolina – sort of – cake. A cooked semolina cake soaked in simple syrup, this bright dessert has both the texture and the flavours to make it the perfect way to unwind on a dreary winter's night.

**SERVING SIZE**

Serves 6–8

**BASIC RECIPES USED**

1 recipe Simple Sugar Syrup
(refer to page 16)

| | | |
|---|---|---|
| coarse semolina | 600 g | 3⅓ cups |
| unsweetened, super fine coconut shreds | 40 g | 4 tbsp |
| ghee | 170 g | ¾ cup |
| full cream milk | 280 ml | 1¼ cups |
| honey | 340 g | 1 cup |

**TO GARNISH**

| | | |
|---|---|---|
| raw halved almonds, skin peeled, or hazelnuts | 65 g | ½ cup |

prepare the syrup and set aside to cool

Preheat the oven to 200°C (392°F).

Prepare a round 24 cm (9 in) tray and grease with ghee.

In a large bowl, combine semolina and coconut, and set aside.

In a small saucepan, melt the ghee. Add the ghee to the dry ingredients, mixing well until all ingredients are incorporated.

In the same saucepan, heat the milk, add the honey and mix until the honey is dissolved.

Then pour it on the semolina mixture and mix just until incorporated.

Feel the mixture with your hands. It should feel smooth with no lumps.

Pour the mixture onto the prepared tray and evenly distribute the mixture to fit the tray.

Brush the top of the mixture with a little bit of ghee.

Spread the almonds or hazelnuts on top of the mixture to decorate it.

Let the mixture set in the refrigerator for about 10 minutes.

Bake for about 30 minutes till it starts to become a golden-brown colour and the edges slightly darker than the centre.

As soon as you remove it from the oven, pour the cooled sugar syrup all over the tray. The syrup should soak in right away. Allow to completely cool.

**TIPS AND TRICKS**

*Once you add the semolina to the mixture make sure you don't over-mix it as it can become hard and lumpy. Mix till it is just incorporated.*

# Cinnamon Biscuits

Aah, the flavour of cinnamon … My mother tells me these were the best biscuits her aunt Saadia used to make! She had a secret that made them so fluffy and dissolved in the mouth. She tells me that the way her aunt shaped the biscuits and packed them in a box was like a machine made them! They looked so perfect; they tasted so divine!

## SERVING SIZE

Serves 10–12

Yields about 45 cookies

| | | |
|---|---|---|
| all purpose flour | 260 g | 2 cups |
| baking powder | 5 g | 1 tsp |
| cinnamon powder | 5 g | 1 tsp |
| unsalted butter | 80 g | ⅓ cup |
| powdered sugar | 140 g | 1 cup + 1 tbsp |
| eggs | 100 g | 2 large |
| vanilla extract | 5 g | 1 tsp |

## SERVING AND STORING SUGGESTIONS

They will last in an airtight container for up to 10 days.

Preheat the oven to 180°C (356°F).

Prepare 2 baking trays lined with parchment paper.

In a bowl, sift together the flour, baking powder and cinnamon.

In a hand-held electric mixer with the paddle attachment, beat the butter and sugar on medium-high speed for about 3 minutes until light and fluffy.

Switch speed to slow and add the eggs one at a time, followed by the vanilla extract.

Add the sifted dry ingredients, until everything is just incorporated.

Dust the palms of your hands with a little flour so the dough doesn't stick and shape the dough in round balls, each around 5 cm (2 in).

Place on prepared baking sheet keeping them about 2 cm (1 in) apart.

Use the back of a round flat surface (like a cup) and press lightly on the cookies to flatten out the balls a little bit and to bake a decorative shape.

Bake for around 15–20 minutes until golden brown.

Allow to cool completely before storing.

### TIPS AND TRICKS

*It's important to sift the dry ingredients very well, a few times over, to get smooth, buttery biscuits.*

### VARIATIONS

Add 10 g (1 tbsp) of unsweetened cocoa powder with the dry ingredients for a chocolate cinnamon cookie.

Alternatively, use 160 g (½ cup) of any choice of jam. Once dough is formed into balls, press with your thumb to have a little dent. Add a teaspoon of jam.

# Kahk (Eid Cookies)

A kahk is a small circular biscuit eaten across the Arab world to celebrate Eid al-Fitr and Easter. It is covered with powdered sugar and can be stuffed with agameya (a mixture of honey, nuts and ghee), lokum, walnuts, pistachios or dates or simply served plain.

Date-filled kahk are believed to be the origin of ma'amoul, a similar Eid biscuit eaten in the Levant. This dish also popular in Indonesia and called as kue kaak as result of acculturation between Arabs and Indonesian. Usually served during Mawlid or Eid al-Fitr.

**SERVING SIZE**

Serves 30–35

Yields about 65 cookies

| | | |
|---|---|---|
| melted ghee | 250 g | 1¼ cups |
| full cream milk | 100 ml | ½ cup |
| active dry yeast | 5 g | 1 tsp |
| all-purpose flour | 500 g | 3¾ cups |
| powdered sugar | 40 g | 4 tbsp |
| kahk essence (if available) | 10 g | 2 tsp |
| vanilla sugar | 2 g | ½ tsp |
| toasted sesame | 10 g | 2 tsp |

Preheat oven to 160°C (320°F).

Prepare 2 baking trays lined with parchment paper.

Begin by preparing all the fillings you choose. Always start with the agameya filling (find recipe below) as it needs time to cool.

Melt the ghee and set it aside.

Warm milk, add in the yeast to milk and set aside.

Place the dry ingredients in a bowl of a stand mixer with the paddle attachment.

Add the ghee and mix on medium speed for about 3 minutes until the ghee is well incorporated and the mixture is creamy and smooth.

Switch to slow speed, gradually pouring in the warmed milk.

Continue mixing for another 2 minutes until the dough is formed.

As soon as dough is formed, stop the mixer.

Scoop a tablespoon-sized dough with the palm of your hand and roll the dough into a ball, using your thumb to press the centre of the ball to make space for the filling. (If you are not using filling, then do not do this step.)

Start adding in the filling of your choice (recipes on the next page) to the centre, then close off the centre by rolling up the dough from the sides of each cookie to completely cover the filling.

Once more, roll with the palms of both hands into a ball.

Place the cookies on to the prepared baking trays about 2 cm (1 in) apart.

Finally, using the back of a fork, make an × (cross) imprint in the cookies to give them a design.

Bake in the preheated oven for about 20–25 minutes until they turn a light golden colour.

*Continued >*

Let them cool for about 10 minutes, then transfer to a wire rack to completely cool.

Using a sieve, dust the tops of the cookies with powdered sugar until completely covered.

## FILLINGS

### FILLING 1: AGAMEYA

| | | |
|---|---|---|
| ghee | 30 g | 3 tbsp |
| all-purpose flour | 20 g | 2 tbsp |
| honey | 340 g | 1 cup |
| toasted sesame seeds | 15 g | 1½ tbsp |
| chopped raw walnuts | 120 g | 1 cup |

Put the ghee into a saucepan on medium heat until melted.

Add flour, stirring continuously, until the mixture turns into a light golden colour.

Add the honey and continue mixing.

Once the mixture starts boiling, continue to stir on the heat for a couple more minutes until it just starts to thicken.

When it thickens, immediately remove from heat.

To know if it is ready, take the back of a teaspoon and dip a little bit of the honey mixture in cold water. If it holds its shape, then it is ready.

Once removed from heat, add in the sesame and walnuts and mix until well incorporated.

Immediately transfer to a separate bowl and refrigerate until it cools down. It should start to firm up, but remain pliable.

Once cooled, put a little bit of ghee on your hands and use the palm of your hands to roll the mixture into bite-sized balls.

Place them on a baking tray lined with parchment paper or greased with ghee and dusted with a flour.

Keep them refrigerated until your cookies are ready to be filled.

Continued >

| | | |
|---|---|---|
| ghee | 10 g | 1 tbsp |
| soft date paste | 500 g | 2 cups |
| cinnamon powder | 5 g | 1 tsp |
| cardamom powder | 2 g | ½ tsp |

## FILLING 2: AGWA (DATE PASTE)

Melt the ghee, but don't let it get too hot.

Knead the date paste with the ghee by hand and add in the rest of the ingredients.

Keep kneading for a minute or 2, or till it is pliable.

Apply a little bit of ghee on your hands and use the palm of your hands to roll the mixture into bite-sized balls.

Line them on parchment paper on a baking tray and keep refrigerated until your cookies are ready to fill.

## TIPS AND TRICKS

*In case kahk essence is not available, you can replace with 1 tsp (5 ml) rose water or just omit all together.*

*When making the dough, once everything is mixed and the dough starts to look smooth, take a small piece with the palm of your hands and make a ball and press on it lightly. If it cracks, then you need to mix the dough a little longer.*

*When decorating the cookies, be very careful with the filled ones as the dough can easily crack.*

*Once the cookies turn light golden in the oven, remove right away to make sure the fillings on the inside remain soft and chewy.*

*Make sure the cookies are completely cool before dusting with sugar, otherwise the cookies will absorb all the sugar.*

***Agameya:** Be careful not to over-cook the honey-ghee mix so it doesn't harden. It needs to remain soft (pliable).*

***Agwa:** If the date paste is hard, add a little more ghee, a teaspoon at a time until it softens.*

My mom's favorite family portrait.

# Conclusion

This book has been a dream of mine for years. I have toyed with it, left it aside as other things became priorities, created it in my mind a hundred times over and then set it aside again. It is finally here and to see it come to life is surreal. I can only hope I have been able to relay my message to all of you with the same amount of love and passion I have towards every single recipe in this book.

My intention is to revive bonding, love, appreciation and connection throughout generations of families. And what better way is there other than making memories through food! I can only hope that this little dream of mine builds its own family of readers that can connect together; I would love to invite you to be in touch with me through our website and social media pages. I would love to hear your feedback and to answer any questions. I wholeheartedly believe that food is a big connector. So, let's connect!

My mom enjoying her mother's baking

# About the Author

Iman Osman has been a baker since learning at her Egyptian Grandmother's knee. She strongly believes in the connection and family bonding that cooking together can bring.

Iman started her career with a small bake shop that sold freshly baked cookies and brownies. She has now expanded and co-owns with her sister, a company producing healthy breakfast cereals and baked goods to provide healthier, safer options to families. Much like the passion put into her book, her business is driven by the passion she has for everything to be "made from scratch" – no additives, no preservatives – just good fresh baking, the old-fashioned way.

My mom (in white on the right side) and my grandma
by her side (left) celebrating my mom's birthday
with my grandma's famous birthday buffets.

# Index

**Publishing information**
Publishing, design, and production facilitated by Passionpreneur Publishing,
A division of Passionpreneur Organization Pty Ltd,
ABN: 48640637529

www.PassionpreneurPublishing.com
Melbourne, VIC | Australia

Ingram Content Group UK Ltd.
Milton Keynes UK
UKHW052150260323
419190UK00001B/1